GOZO

Is the Grass Greener?

OTHER BOOKS BY FREYA BARRINGTON

The #1 UK 2015 Bestseller in Social Work Category

Known to Social Services

GOZO

Is the Grass Greener?

Freya Barrington

First published in 2015 by
FARAXA

Published by
FARAXA Publishing
38 Antonio Nani Street, Rabat RBT 3047, Malta; and
P. O. Box 37, East Longmeadow, MA 01020, USA.
http://faraxapublishing.com
info@faraxapublishing.com

ISBN 978-9995748-25-8

Printed in the United States of America.

To the wonderful people of Gozo and
the lifelong friends we made there

ACKNOWLEDGEMENTS

In writing any book, there are people along the way who knowingly or otherwise, contribute to the work. Such is the case with *Gozo; Is the Grass Greener?*

I am indebted to my husband, Steve, who offered his unconditional love and encouragement once again. I am also indebted to our sadly missed lurchers, Ollie and Ralph, who provided me with so much love and material, and who come alive again through the pages of this book.

Special thanks must go to all our wonderful friends in Gozo, whose influence and input are woven throughout this story. A big thank you goes to Mark Cassar for his part in the story and to Manwel Zammit, our manager and dear friend, thank you for everything.

I am particularly pleased that the illustration on the front cover has been designed by Michael Martin. Michael illustrates Alex Graham's *Fred Basset* and has provided a wickedly accurate illustration for *Gozo: Is the Grass Greener?* It is exactly as I imagined it would be: perfect. Many thanks, Michael.

Thank you to our good friend, Neil Whittaker, for sharing his amazing photographic skills and providing beautiful shots of Gozo for this book. Thank you also for the wedding photos to our dear friend, Jeff Cox, who has now sadly passed away.

Finally, a wholehearted thank you goes to Faraxa Publishing for supporting me by publishing this work, in particular to the director, Joanne Micallef.

Hay field in Gozo

CONTENTS

FOREWORD

What would persuade a (normally) fairly sensible woman to walk out on 27 years of marriage, become a professional singer, marry a man who performs as Elvis and move 1700 miles to another country – where, by the way, she became a bestselling author? Curious? Then read on . . . . .

Statistics indicate that there are certain life events more stressful than others. In the top 10 of stressful events are moving house, divorce, marriage, illness and the death of a loved one. Between 2006 and 2015, my husband, Steve, and I lived through all of the above in one form or another, along with a host of other interesting experiences. From such a personal history, I have created a story that I hope will resonate with you and have wide appeal. Who among us has not known the heady excitement of a new love or the tragedy of bereavement? The joy of owning a pet or the bitterness of divorce?

Gozo: Is the Grass Greener? is a book about love and life. It is not intended to be a travel guide about the island of Gozo in the Maltese archipelago. It is an honest book, written from all our years of personal experiences, with a narrative of events – some humorous, some sad or serious – all recounted with candour and sincerity. In it, a question is raised: *Is the Grass Greener?* Not only in relation to moving to another country, but in our newly formed relationship.

There are many reflective anecdotes, which provide background to the story. We make the leap from singing on the circuits of club land in the UK, to singing under the stars on a Maltese island only 3.5 miles square. We move away from the stresses of the rat race in England, to a gentler and more peaceful way of life among the welcoming people of Gozo. We experience highs and lows as we adjust to our new life, making good friends along the way.

Through my writing, Steve shares his painful struggle with the depressive side of bipolar disorder and I reflect upon my unexpected role of carer.

On a lighter note, you can read about many of the unique and often humorous experiences we had day-to-day, which left us smiling and saying, "Only in Gozo."

Gozo as an island has seen a marked rise in visits from tourists, some more famous than others. The tiny bay of Mġarr ix-Xini, which was one of our favourite haunts, was, at the time of writing, used as a film set for Brad Pitt and Angelina Jolie's latest movie. If you have never been to this jewel of an island, it is my sincere hope that in reading this book, you may decide to see it for yourself.

For now, I invite you to discover whether or not, for us, the grass really *was* greener.

Freya Barrington

GOZO

Is the Grass Greener?

On the bike in Gozo

CHAPTER 1

March 2010

I guess when it came down to it, I had Sky TV to thank for our decision to move to the beautiful island of Gozo, part of the archipelago of the Maltese Islands in the Mediterranean; although it could just as easily have been BT, British Gas, Orange, O2, Severn Trent Water or any of the other utilities and 'services' I had done battle with over the phone. In the end, the final straw award went to Sky TV. Let me explain.

The day began like any other day. It was raining, cold, dark and miserable. I had a to-do list which included phoning up Sky TV as they had charged me for additional channels I knew for a fact that I had cancelled. You know the kind of thing I mean: they ring you up, offer you three months 'free' movie channels and as long as you cancel by a certain date, there is no charge. The only catch is that if you are anything like me, you inevitably forget and end up with charges. There then follows a three hour phone call or more to a call centre 5000 miles away and a great deal of hassle to cancel the free offer.

On the day in question, I had received such a call and laughed. I distinctly remember the laughing part: it was a kind of wise, all-knowing laugh with a sarcastic edge.

"Oh, I don't think so," I added in case the woman failed to interpret the subtlety of my laugh. "I've done this before and got caught out. You see, I always forget to cancel it and end up getting charged."

I could positively hear the woman consulting her crib sheet of *Ready-made answers for disgruntled customers.*

"No, no, ma'am. This won't happen," she soothed. "You see, we'll write to you 10 days before the date so you won't forget."

I paused.

"Really?" I asked. "You'll actually write to me, to remind me?"

The woman could hear me wavering from 5000 miles distant and she knew she had me.

"Of course, ma'am. We understand about our customers forgetting, so we'll do this for you. There's no need to worry."

I considered this option and had to admit that it seemed pretty failsafe. I mean, I was going to get a letter, the nice lady said. Hook. Line. Sinker. She reeled me in with relatively little effort.

However, determined not to get caught out, I got my 2010 Elvis diary and wrote under 2nd June, in a gold sparkly pen, *CANCEL SKY*. Ha! NOW I would be sure to remember. I sat back smugly and got ready to enjoy three months of free movies, confident in the knowledge that they would truly be free, this time around. And I would wait for the nice lady to write.

The 2nd June eventually arrived. The movies had been watched, enjoyed and discussed. Not least in the discussions featured the marvellous freeness of it all. I noted with mild irritation that the nice lady seemed to have forgotten to send me the letter, but never mind. I had it all written down in my Elvis diary, with a gold sparkly pen, so I initiated the call to cancel.

Now, if you ever had the misfortune of having to ring up Sky TV, you know the drill: press #1 if you want to subscribe and we will answer your call double quick to take your money. But if you press any other number, we know that means:

a) You have a problem;

b) You wish to complain;

c) You wish to cancel your subscription.

As we have no interest whatsoever in dealing with any of those issues, we will make you wait upwards of 40 minutes to demonstrate our chagrin, in the hope that you will:

a) Lose the will to live;

b) Give up;

c) Hang up and continue to let us take your money.

As I wanted to cancel something, I had to endure the obligatory wait, complete with increasingly annoying messages telling me just how important my call was and how valuable a customer I was. Like many of you, I am sure, I found myself yelling into the phone.

"I'm not THAT important, am I? No, I've been on hold for 20 minutes now. No, I don't want to visit your website. I want someone with skin on, to pick up the phone."

Usually, when I am in full rant, someone will answer with a smooth, "I'm sorry to have kept you waiting."

And like most of the population, I will respond, "Oh, it's okay. No problem."

That is due to fear – fear that if any manner of complaint is voiced, it will result in the person hanging up and I will have to start over, like a bad game of *Snakes and Ladders*.

Eventually, I got through that day, although my jaws were aching from the amount of passive-aggressive teeth grinding. But I got through. I explained my situation and was told that the movie package had been cancelled. I needed to do nothing else.

"Are you sure?" I asked, nervously. "You see, I've had this before and you've gone on and charged me."

Off the receiver at the other end went into another soothing speech.

"No, no, ma'am. There's no need for concern. It's cancelled now, it's all taken care of."

I remained sceptical.

"You've made a note of it then?" I reiterated.

"Ma'am, I'm looking at your screen right now. Hear me typing, it's done."

I strained my ears and fancied I could hear a faint tapping.

"Oh, okay, but you didn't write to me like you said you would," I added somewhat petulantly.

"Is there anything else I can help you with, ma'am?" asked the voice from far away.

"No, that's it. But I hope it's cancelled as I'm going to be really annoyed if I have to ring up again."

Five thousand miles away, the woman trotted out a final affirmation.

"I assure you, ma'am, it's done."

I got the Elvis diary out again. To be sure, I made a note of the day and time I made this call – good job that I did. You know what is coming, don't you?

~ ~ ~ ~ ~

They charged me! With a wearyingly depressing inevitability, they charged me!

The trouble was because I paid by direct debit and because I banked online and did not get statements, and because I did not check my bank account, they managed to wangle two months of payments out of me before I noticed. Needless to say, I got on the phone again, indignation at an all-time high. Of course, I had to repeat the painful charade, only this time in triplicate. My middle-aged, grumpy old woman rage was unsurpassed and I was passed around a variety of people before I finally got hold of a supervisor. Our discussion went something like this:

Me: "I knew this would happen, I knew you'd charge me. I was told someone would write to me, to remind me about this."

Supervisor: "Ma'am, it's not our policy to write to people, to remind them to cancel their subscriptions."

Me: "Whaaat?!"

Supervisor: "Ma'am, we have millions of customers. We could not possibly write to them all to give reminders."

Me: "But I was definitely told by someone that I'd get a letter 10 days prior to the date I had to cancel."

Supervisor: "I'm sorry, ma'am, but it's not our policy to write to customers in this way."

Me: "Well, someone DID tell me that. But, anyway, it's irrelevant. I have the date here in my Elvis diary. I rang on 2nd June, spoke to someone and cancelled this. And now you've carried on and charged me, which I knew full well you would."

Supervisor (pretending to consult the screen): "I'm sorry, ma'am. We have no record of a call from you on 2nd June or any other date. This is why you've been charged as you haven't cancelled by the due date."

By now, the whole scenario was like a very bad movie. I felt as if the entire situation was a conspiracy to drive me over the edge – no doubt orchestrated by my ex. It was a test to see how long it would take me to turn into Michael Douglas in *Falling Down* where he loses control and shoots everyone in sight. I opened my mouth, but no words came out; they had literally failed me. I felt my blood pressure rising and a pulse in my neck, and another at the corner of my eye, beginning to jump – and I knew, in that very moment, how crimes of passion were committed.

Eventually, I got a grip on my sanity and the conversation continued:

Me: "You're lying! I know you're lying and you know you're lying! You say you record all phone calls? Right, I insist you go through every call made on 2nd June until you find mine, because I know I rang."

Supervisor: "Ma'am, even if we did find a record of the call, you would not be privy to that information."

Me (slightly strangled): "What?!"

Supervisor: "I'm sorry, ma'am, but there would be a £10 surcharge for you to listen to any calls made to Sky TV."

Me: "Are you making this up?? Let me get this straight: if you discover I DID make a call cancelling the movie channel, you won't let me listen to it? And to actually listen to it, when you found it, you'd make me pay even more money??"

Supervisor: "That's correct, madam, you're not privy to that information unless you choose to pay the surcharge."

And that was it, RIGHT THERE, the straw that broke the camel's back. That sanctimonious *That's correct, ma'am; blah, blah, blah* . . . . . that was the one. I knew I was utterly and completely done with the UK, but not before I rightfully received a refund from Sky TV . . . . . well . . . . .

Hell hath no fury like a woman kept on hold.

Chapter 2

August 2010

So why Gozo? Of all the places in the world, Gozo? We had been told that we would love it and were assured that our first experience of the magical island of Calypso as it is sometimes known, would be unforgettable. After all there was beautiful weather, friendly and welcoming people, it was not expensive to eat out and had a charm of its own. Having visited the main island of Malta in the archipelago on three occasions without a hop-over visit to Gozo, we were encouraged to try out this tiny jewel in the Mediterranean as a standalone holiday destination. We were assured it was quieter and less crowded than its big sister, Malta. Yes, it would be a truly unforgettable experience.

Thus in August 2010, we agreed that we would rent an apartment in Gozo for a week and after some internet searching, we settled on the sleepy-looking Xlendi Bay. We also agreed that we would take Steve's 14-year-old daughter, Sabrina, with us. Unforgettable? We had absolutely no idea what we were in for.

I pause here to shake my head and sigh at the foolishness of that particular decision. Anyone out there with a teenager will no doubt be shaking their head and possibly even wincing as they marvel at our naiveté. Did we really think that we could take an almost stereotypically perfect example of a dissatisfied generation to a small, quiet island where free wi-fi was as remote a possibility as my ever becoming a size 8 again? – bar the starvation diet, of course, where I *could* actually make it down to an 8. Like most teenagers, Sabrina had a serious dependence bordering on addiction to internet social websites – not to mention her iPhone, laptop, iPod and junk food. *What were we thinking?!*

In hindsight, it was not the best decision we ever made. Mainland Spain or even Florida in the States would have been better options here, but

Gozo it was. And I omitted to mention that in addition to the addiction to all things internet, we had four years of stored up, brooding resentment directed at myself as her dad's evil, new partner who had ruined her life, to add to the mix.

Anyway, as a glass-half-full kind of person, I was determined to make the best of it, so I set about planning and organising the flights, transfers and so on that accompany any holiday. Steve was texting Sabrina regularly to advise her of what she needed to bring along – lots of swimwear, shorts, tee shirts, something to go out in at night; that sort of thing. He would send her long lists of things needed, painstakingly spelling out every word in longhand as all adults of a certain age tend to do. The texts that came back without fail, however, would just say:

> *K.*

"K?" Steve would ask me with a frown. "What the hell is K?"

"I think she means okay, darling. She's agreeing with you," I would explain.

"Well, why doesn't she say so then?" would come the scowling, Neanderthal reply.

"It's just the way they communicate, darling. It's shorthand," I would add.

"Well, it's stupid," he would growl in return.

I was already captivated by the photographs of Gozo, with its hidden coves and bays, and the crystal clear waters surrounding it. I could almost taste that local cuisine: the pizzas handmade in front of you, the locally produced wines and cheeses . . . . . mmm, it was going to be a treat! I wondered vaguely if Sabrina would eat *ġbejniet* – goat's cheese.

The earliest hint of real things to come was when we got to the airport. It transpired that despite her father's longwinded, repeated, clear texts of instructions as to what to bring, Sabrina did not, in fact, possess a bikini or swimming costume of any kind – not that pencil thin, teenage girls wear swimming costumes, but you know . . . . . Sabrina announced the issue with that marvellously sullen, stone face which humans only possess between the ages of 13 and 17 years – dead eyed, expressionless and said in a manner which somehow managed to apportion blame to both her dad and myself.

Steve's response was to ask me, "Can we sort something out for her?"

My response, however, was to look as if I had just begun to suck a lemon. Actually, it was more like two lemons, a grapefruit and a generous slice of lime.

I took a deep breath to prevent words coming out such as, "Why, WHY don't you have a bikini with you?! I mean your dad told you enough times to bring one."

I avoided saying such things for two reasons:

1. The words would fall on deaf ears; and
2. It would not have made the slightest difference.

Instead, I swallowed the cocktail of citrus fruit and propelled said teenager towards one of the airport boutiques. Now, for those of you who have never had the dubious pleasure of shopping in an airport boutique, a word of warning: any sign which reads *DUTY FREE* is to be ignored. It is a lie; a complete lie. It should be translated as follows:

"This is probably the most expensive shop you've ever been into. You cannot possibly afford anything in here and the experience will leave you penniless for the rest of your holiday."

In my life, I have had to stop going into those brightly lit, wonderfully smelling and alluring shops, which drew me like the proverbial moth to a flame, as I was heard to say loudly:

"Duty Free? Duty Free?? I can get this cheaper at *Boots the Chemist*. Look at the price of this *Toblerone*! And *Tesco's* are doing a 2-for-1 on this. £10! £10 for a box of *Roses*! I don't think so."

You get the picture, right?

Anyway, I digress – and we had not even left the UK yet. There we were in exactly such an establishment, waited on by women who looked as if they had applied an entire box of *Elizabeth Arden* product to their faces in one go. The chosen bikini resembled a plaited bootlace crossed with a spider's web – and it cost £35. I tried hard not to imagine what a similar item might have cost at *Primark* or *TK Maxx*, but I could not help it.

As we left the shop, Sabrina's internal fashion radar picked up on a trilby-type hat and I saw the slightest glimmer of light in her eyes. Pouncing on an opportunity to be popular (damn you, repressed Grammar School behaviour patterns), I asked her brightly if she would also like that hat – and just like that, I found myself £55 lighter in total. I strongly suspected that I was no more popular than I had been 10 minutes earlier. But hey, I tried!

Eventually, after the customary three-hour wait at the airport, a flight lasting three hours 20 minutes, a 45-minute taxi transfer to the ferry, a 25-minute ferry ride to Gozo and a final 15-minute ride to the apartment, we arrived. There we also became about another 50 euros poorer as Sabrina possessed a fascinating need to be fed and watered at every available opportunity. I began wondering if she had an inbuilt sense of an impending, worldwide food shortage or something as I had never witnessed a child, a teenager, with quite such a capacity for junk food.

There had been an almost non-stop mantra of, "I'm hungry, I need a drink."

It started at the airport, continued on the plane, picked up again at the airport in Malta, progressed in the taxi and reached a finale on the ferry to Gozo. Add to that the inevitable, "Are we nearly there?" and you will get some idea of how frazzled our nerves were by the time we reached our destination.

As ever, words that sprang to mind – which on this occasion were, "How the hell can you still be hungry, you've eaten your own body weight in chicken nuggets?" – were suppressed.

Instead, anxious not to spoil the holiday, I smiled and asked, "What would you like?"

You know that could not last, right? All that repressed rage. It had to come out . . . . . eventually.

I am not going to dwell too much on events which unfolded during that week. It was a bit like *Groundhog Day*, a never-ending loop of:

a) I don't like this/that (*fish in the sea, seaweed, the menu, the heat, Valletta, whatever*);

b) I want egg and chips (*in every single restaurant*);

c) I'm bored;

d) I don't like swimming in the sea (*Of course, you don't!*);

e) This bikini doesn't fit (*I'm sorry, my response to this is censored*);

f) I don't want to do that/go there;

g) I'm bored;

h) Can we go back to the apartment now? (*No!*);

i) I'm sitting next to Dad;

j) My phone's gone flat (*What? You didn't bring a charger? Really? After all those texts your dad sent reminding you to bring one!*);

k) I'm bored;

l) I can't sleep (*Try being quiet*);

m) It's too hot (*It's August in the Med. What did you think?*);

n) I need a drink;

o) I'm hungry;

p) I'm bored;

q) Can I have some money?

You get the picture. The effort of suppressing my murderous emotions became a daily battle. On one occasion, I had to go for a long walk, during which time I marched around like a demented marionette and actually had a panic attack with the enormity of the task of holding it all in. By day four, Steve was apologising.

Through clenched teeth, I was saying things such as, "Do NOT, under any circumstances, ask me to do this EVER AGAIN!"

One day, it was agreed that Sabrina could have 10 euros to spend. However, she asked if we could keep it for her until she returned home and get £10 sterling instead. Okay, I could go for that (*watch this space*). I remember so clearly the day I finally cracked. We had been sitting outside a hotel on the waterfront having a drink, with the usual echo from Sabrina:

"I'm still thirsty, can I have another?"

I had gone inside to check out the rooms and to take an opportunity for some solitary hyperventilation. I was determined that Steve and I would return *alone* to relax and have a holiday which did not involve being pecked to death 24/7. When I emerged, Steve informed me that Sabrina had asked where I went, so he had explained to her that we might return for another holiday.

Her response had been, "Yeah, bring me."

That was it! I could feel all the pent up, bikini-buying, week-of-complaining rage coming up like a volcano. And it all come out.

"WHAAAT?! Bring you with us? Bring *you* with us?? Are you serious?? I am never, NEVER bringing you on holiday again as long as I live and breathe! You've done nothing but complain the whole time; nothing suits you."

I suspect my eyes were bulging at that point and I think I spat out at least once. Anyway, I was certainly not done yet. I continued ranting and raving about teenagers in general, my lack of finances following the trip and on and on and on. When I was done, there was a small silence, after which Sabrina responded with a nonchalant shrug.

"Yeah, well, I only asked," Sabrina continued, "I'm bored on my own. Next time, let me bring a mate with me and it'll be better."

Oh. My. God. Had she really just asked me to let her bring along another teenager? That provoked a fresh outburst.

I spluttered, "Bring a mate? Bring a mate??" (I seemed to need to say a lot of things twice). "Why on EARTH would I do that? It's bad enough with one teenager, never mind two of you! Oh yeah, let me bring TWO teenagers on holiday, then I can really have a nervous breakdown!"

Steve sat quietly through it all with that bemused look men get. He said nothing, but was thinking *I wonder why this is happening?* The reality of it all was that it had, in the main, passed him totally by. However, by the last evening of our holiday, Steve too snapped after a particularly tricky evening during which he had, against his better judgement, allowed Sabrina to have a cocktail (*bad idea*). Steve had bundled his daughter back to the flat with the accompanying warning:

"And I don't want to hear another peep out of you all night, do you understand?"

I patted his arm in silent sympathy as Steve lay rigidly in bed staring at the ceiling, quietly hyperventilating (*it really did help*).

Somehow, we got through the journey home, albeit with lots more feeding and watering along the way. We eventually got to the moment of dropping Sabrina off. As she got out of the car, she turned to me and cleared her throat. *Ah,* I thought, *she's going to apologise for her behaviour or, at least, say thank you for the holiday.*

But Sabrina looked at me. Just as cool as you like, she said:

"You owe me a tenner."

My nervous breakdown was complete.

CHAPTER 3

December 2005

It was the first week in December and I was feeling anything but festive. I was 27 years into a marriage in which I had been shamefully neglected and, I suspected, cheated on. The relationship had been shipwrecked one dark, stormy night many years ago, hitting the sharp, jagged rocks of reality where it foundered and gave up. Trouble was, no one knew how to get off. The lifeboats were missing and it seemed that I was trapped on the doomed vessel for the rest of my life. In short, I was miserable and very lonely. Of course, I had contemplated leaving many times, but my mother's words about the grass not necessarily being greener on the other side had a tendency to float into my head and serve as a deterrent. In addition, the prospect of trying to start a new life all over was daunting and seemingly unrealistic. Questions such as how on earth would I manage financially and where would I go, were left unanswered. And so it continued: two strangers occupying the same space.

My three daughters were grown up and quite rightly all doing their own thing, giving me one less reason to stay. I was dreading another Christmas which, I knew from bitter experience, would be filled with sickening pretence and stifling insincerity. I wondered how much longer I could keep up the charade and knew that after all the years of make-believe, the façade was about to crack. I had reached the end of a very short rope. I could not go on, but the future seemed obscure, anonymous and more than a little frightening. However, surely anything had to be better than that? One of my two faithful lurchers sensed my mood and came over to push his long, pointy nose anxiously into my lap.

"Hey, buddy," I said, grateful for the attention. "How you doing?"

Six-year-old Ralph wagged furiously at the reciprocal attention. A huge, leggy cartoon of a dog, he was loyal and loving, and along with his older, wiser and somewhat tatty, 15-year-old, big brother, Ollie, they kept me sane. Walking them was my escape and we would wander miles in each other's company across the beautiful, rolling hills of the Peak District where I spent more and more of my time. The affectionate interchange was disrupted when the phone rang. It was my eldest daughter, Steff. The sound of her voice brought an immediate smile to my face – it always cheered me up to hear from her.

"Hey, what's new?" I asked, shaking off the blues which threatened to overwhelm me.

"Hey, Mum," Steff began, brightly. "It's my friend's birthday this Friday and he's having a private party with an Elvis guy singing. You have to come."

I hesitated. I really was not one for socialising, especially as a couple. And an Elvis guy? Hmm, not sure about that. I mean, I adore Elvis – who doesn't? But I had yet to see anyone who could do him justice.

"I don't know, Steff," I began, stalling for time.

But she interrupted me.

"Mummm," she pleaded with all the finesse of a five-year-old. "You have to come, it'll be no good if you don't," she wheedled.

I caved in. It would be worth it to spend time with my lovely girl.

"Oh, okay then," I conceded. "What time?

And just like that, my destiny was sealed.

Looking back, I think that the gods, whoever they were, must have glanced down and condescended to break the spell of unhappiness by working some magic on my behalf. I imagined them smiling as they whispered the details of their conspiracy among themselves, agreeing that *It is time* . . . . . and it was.

Friday, 8th December, 2005 will be eternally engraved in my mind as the day that changed my life forever. I got ready to go out as agreed, but as usual we were running famously late. Call it what you will, but I recognised it from bitter experience as passive-aggressive behaviour. Knowing we needed to be at a certain place, for a certain time, my then husband would take great delight in ensuring that we were late, especially if the occasion was important to me. In any event, we set off eventually, with me being in an all-too-familiar haze of unspoken resentment and irritation. We arrived as the "Elvis guy" was in full flow. I do not recall what he was singing and I do not really recall who else was there. I do, however, recall stopping dead in my tracks almost as soon as I got through the door and feeling that I had been hit fully in the face with a fairly sizeable shovel.

I stared in utter fascination at that man who was, quite simply, the best-looking individual I had ever seen in my life. It was not just his good looks which stopped me in my tracks. He had a tremendous charisma which emanated from him in waves; an almost hypnotic, Svengali-like persona which was so unique I could not move. I was transfixed by that guy and just stood there like a plank, staring and feeling acutely self-conscious. That was just not me. I was not given to ogling men or even noticing if they were good looking. At that point in life, I had just about resigned myself to a future of solitude, dog-walking, bird-watching and, possibly, even wearing tweed. I would, no doubt, end up being "that crazy old woman" who wandered around the village with her two big dogs, talking to anyone who cared to listen to her ramblings.

Steff spotted me and shouted, "Yay, my mum's here!"

At that point, the Elvis guy stopped singing and said in a voice which sounded like velvet, "Don't you mean your sister?"

It was as corny a line as any I had ever heard, but the impact on me was akin to plunging into a pool of cold water on a hot day. My heart began to pound. I blushed like a schoolgirl and my throat went dry. Just like that, people, I was in love.

Somehow, I found a seat and sat down in a kind of stupid trance. I simply could not take my eyes of that man. I felt embarrassed and was sure that every single person in the room knew how I felt. I was mesmerised by him, but my fascination turned quickly to horror as I saw him working his way through the crowd towards me. As he got closer, I could smell his aftershave which was divine. Closer still and I was frozen like a deer in the headlights of a car, staring into the most beautiful, brown eyes I had ever seen. They were like melted chocolate. I sunk down in my seat willing him to stay, but at the same time wishing he would go as I was certain he had read my mind. In the distance, I heard Steff laugh.

"Look at my mum, he's singing to her and she doesn't know what to do."

You got that right, I thought, struggling to control my breathing as that Elvis guy did, indeed, sing to me. Then he was gone. I felt an immediate, totally inappropriate mixture of emotions: I felt bereft and cheated at the same time. I watched as the Elvis guy continued working the room and I experienced an unreasonable stab of jealousy as he sung to other women in the way he had sung to me. *When did I become Shirley Valentine?* I thought, wryly.

I loved singing and someone, at some point unbeknown to me, asked the Elvis guy if I could go up and sing with him – and he agreed. Looking back, I realise how unusual the whole situation was as it was not karaoke and people did not just get up and 'have a go.' When the news was relayed to me that the Elvis guy had agreed that I could sing with him, I was mortified and immediately refused to consider it. However, the lure of being in close proximity to that enigma of a man was irresistibly tempting. The deciding factor was hearing the bitterly sarcastic voice of my then husband who was holding court. He was telling anyone who cared to listen:

"Oh, here we go. She thinks she can sing."

And similar words of great discouragement.

It was the kick I needed. *I'll show you*, I thought, as I plucked up all my courage, sank a large glass of *Sauvignon Blanc* and declared:

"I'll do it."

And I did.

In the interval, I went to speak to the Elvis guy who, I learned, was called Steve. He smiled easily as he spoke to me and, for some reason, I had a sudden image of a lion: honey-eyed, majestic and watchful.

"So what shall we sing?" he asked. "What do you know?"

All I could do was stare and mumble and feel completely ridiculous as I soaked up the waves of gorgeousness emanating from Steve. If he was the lion, I was undoubtedly the unsuspecting gazelle about to be taken down. I was tongue-tied, awkward and behaving like a love-struck teenager. *Pull yourself together*, I told myself. *He'll think you're an idiot.*

After some debate, we agreed to sing *In the Ghetto* as I vaguely knew the words. How I managed to get through it, I will never know, but at the end of my lacklustre performance, Steve was all encouragement and asked me if I had ever considered singing professionally. Naturally, I thought he was being sarcastic, but Steve was deadly serious and told me that if I ever needed any help to get started, that I should ring him up. Very deliberately, Steve then took my hand and kissed it. As he stood up again, he looked at me with those impossibly brown eyes and said with utter sincerity:

"I think you're very beautiful."

I almost fainted. It was not happening, it could not be happening. No one had ever said that to me in my entire life. I was sadly unaccustomed to receiving compliments of any sort from my so-called husband. The most I had ever got was way back in 1982, when he once said that I looked nice. But, seriously, that was about it and even that had been offered begrudgingly as I had asked how I looked. And now here was the Elvis guy – this charismatic, handsome man – kissing my hand and offering compliments. You bet, was I swept away by it all!

A fat man once said, "If you don't love your wife, someone else will."

Those words had never held more truth. I returned to my seat floating on air and took great delight in observing my husband, who was looking decidedly put out by the whole thing.

"Are we going?" he asked, petulantly. "I've had enough."

I smiled sweetly and replied, "You go if you want. I'm staying. He's really good."

My husband stayed, of course, sulking for the remainder of the evening, but it was too late. The gods had acted and the die was cast. Somehow, I knew that nothing would ever be the same again. Whatever had just happened, be it for real or part of an act, I had been treated with respect and made to feel I was worth something. Although I knew that I was probably being ridiculous, I had the strangest premonition about that Elvis guy and myself – and unbeknown to me, he was feeling exactly the same way.

Somewhere, far off, the gods gave each other one last, knowing wink and launched the lifeboat.

CHAPTER 4

September 2010

One of the things we did when we arrived in Gozo for the first time in 2010 was to visit a bar/restaurant which provided entertainment in the form of karaoke. It was called *The Captain's Table* and situated in Xlendi Bay. The place was also a hotel and a dive centre. Little did we know at the time, but that unassuming place would be a deciding factor in making our move to Gozo. The place was (and is at the time of writing) owned and run by Mark: a friendly, American guy who lived in Gozo for many years.

Our first impression of *The Captain's Table* was of a cosy, candle-lit, welcoming place where both locals and expats hung out. Mark was keen to promote the place as a live music venue, which also had regular karaoke nights for the many tourists who found their way into the bar. At the time we visited, there really was not much in the way of live entertainment on the island of Gozo and Mark was at the forefront in making efforts to bring about change.

Steve and I had been together for four years at that point. We were engaged to be married. We had met on that fateful day back in 2005 when I went to see him performing at one of his Elvis cabaret shows and the rest, really, was history. It was Steve who had encouraged me to sing professionally and within a few months, I had three agents in various parts of the UK. I was kept extremely busy singing every weekend and loving every minute of it.

I had always loved to sing. I had sung in the school choir, although that was actually a ruse to avoid going to class – which my teachers never did rumble to. My musical talent in school, however, was somewhat suppressed as my music teacher – *Mrs Lewis, where are you now?* – would come into the room and scan the class with eyes like heat-seeking missiles until they landed on me. She would then point her bony finger very deliberately at me and utter one word:

"OUT!"

The reason for that was my seemingly complete inability to sing the correct words to any song. Never exactly a model pupil, I simply *had* to make up ridiculous words and substitute them for the originals. Mrs Lewis would watch me eagle-eyed as the girls in class all dutifully sang along to her terrible, outdated songs. Even when being scrutinised, I could not help but sing my own composition. Consequently, I spent all my years in her class standing in the corridor from the outset of the lesson.

Steve, on the other hand, had been a professional singer for many years. He was an accomplished multi-instrumentalist and published songwriter. He had worked for many years as a session drummer for most of the big bands of the 70's and the 80's, and had become a singer by accident when asked to stand in for someone who had fallen ill. The similarity between Steve's voice and that of Elvis was duly noted and he decided to put his talent to good use. In the UK, Steve had a strong local following and appeared many times on National TV. He was extremely busy and in high demand as an entertainer.

But to return to the original subject, there we were in Gozo on holiday. We decided to visit Mark's bar on karaoke night for a bit of fun, especially as we had Sabrina with us. Like her dad, she had a good voice and loved to sing. I recall singing no more than two songs and had a fun night. As we left, we chatted to Mark who asked if we were professionals. Our cover was blown! In the course of the ensuing conversation, something was said along the lines of:

"Well, if you're ever around this way, come sing for us."

Now, we all know that when on holiday, many things are said. You make friends with people, with whom you vow to keep in touch. You exchange emails, Facebook details, phone numbers even and so on. However, as soon as you are off the plane, you cannot even recall their names. But this . . . . . This was different and we both knew it.

When we got back to the UK, I booked another holiday to Gozo just for Steve and myself. We agreed that we had not really had the opportunity to relax or enjoy the holiday for the reasons stated in Chapter Two. With our trip only a few weeks away, I had an idea. I sent Mark an email and told him that we would soon be returning back to Gozo. I also asked him if he would like us to put on a proper show at his bar. Mark immediately agreed, but he asked us to do three shows, not just one. *Excellent,* I thought. A working holiday is always great fun and we would get to perform in Gozo. So we duly set about organising the logistics of it all. Obviously, we could not take heavy equipment with us, but someone offered to lend us some gear, so we were all set.

We returned to Gozo in September 2010 and to me, it felt like going home. I had only spent one week of my life there, but had already fallen under the spell of that breathtakingly beautiful island. We stayed at *Saint Patrick's Hotel* in Xlendi, in a fifth floor room with an enormous balcony overlooking the heavenly bay. I stood on the balcony greedily drinking it all in. The boats bobbed easily on the clear waters. Tourists wandered along the seafront, cameras in hand, capturing the splendour of it all. The many restaurants and bars were teeming with life as people soaked up the sun and enjoyed the bliss of the tranquil, little bay. They sipped Italian coffee, savoured the local delicacies and wondered why they had never visited before.

I stood looking at the feast of beauty laid out before me and, right there and then, the magic of Gozo slid quietly into my heart. I turned to Steve and spoke with deep conviction.

"I need to live here."

Without missing a beat, my wonderful, marvellous, one-in-a-million fiancé replied:

"Okay. If that's what you want to do, then that's what we'll do."

What a man!

We did the shows and Mark added another one, so in total we did four. Between us, Steve and I sang a lot of 60's, 70's, rock-n-roll, country, Elvis, and so on, all of which seemed to appeal to our audiences who kept returning for more. It was all great fun and we felt a sense of acceptance and friendship from the expats and locals alike, which we had never experienced in the UK.

On one particular night, I noticed a local guy at the bar. He was smiling encouragement at us the whole time. When we took a break, he came over with his faithful cocker spaniel – whom, he said, was called Shadow – and introduced himself as Manwel. He told us that he had an English partner, Honor, who would soon be moving to Gozo. We had no idea at the time that it really *was* the start of a beautiful, enduring friendship. Manwel declared his great faith in us and in our ability to succeed as entertainers in Gozo – and, coming from a local, that was good to hear.

We were overwhelmed by the friendliness of everyone in Gozo. We were also being urged to go and live there, with many people asking for more of our kind of music. Mark generously agreed to book us for further shows in his bar if we did decide to move – that meant we would have work and very welcome income. And as I had already fallen in love with the little island, it took little persuading when someone else mentioned that they knew of a flat in a place called Marsalforn. We could have the flat for a few months if we did decide to go over and use it as base to explore our options, until we made a final decision as to what we wanted to do with our lives. Never one to let the grass grow, we went to see the flat the following day. It had everything we needed, with the added bonus of views of the sea and a roof on which to sunbathe. It was ideal. I turned to Steve:

"What have we got to lose?"

I could see him thinking about it. Moving from one country to another is no small decision, we both knew that.

"The grass is not necessarily any greener here," Steve cautioned.

But I saw something new in his eyes: it was the hope of a better way of life. There was a silence of about 10 seconds, which was all he needed.

"Let's do it," Steve said.

The decision was made. We were going to live in Gozo. We were on our way.

Gozo: is the grass greener?

CHAPTER 5

The decision had been made – we were off to live in Gozo. I am guessing that most, if not all, of you reading this will, at some time or other in your life, have moved house; some more than others. You, therefore, know from experience how stressful it can be. Moving abroad gathers all that stress, screws it into a concentrated ball, then adds things like registration for your car and entry requirements for our beloved lurcher, Ollie, which almost gave me a nervous breakdown – not to mention the route planning which, of course, was a manly task to which Steve readily applied himself. I would find him staring for hours on end at a map of Europe, turning the pages back and forth, nodding slowly or frowning and shaking his head, all the while *hmmm*-ing to himself.

We had decided to drive all the way rather than fly as it would afford us the opportunity of taking a considerable amount of belongings with us. Ollie was also way too old to be put on a plane in a cage and would be better off in the car with us, where we could keep an eye on him. Aahh, Ollie!

If you have never known the sheer delight of owning a lurcher, then you have missed out on one of life's best experiences. The day Ollie came into my life, I had gone to the rescue compound for another dog to add to my menagerie. I was minded to go for a small terrier as my German Shepherd had developed wanderlust and I had reckoned that a small dog would keep her company, deterring her from going AWOL. Ollie's was the first kennel one reached at the compound and upon hearing visitors, he jumped up on his back legs, looked into me with those big, brown eyes (not *at* me, you understand, but *into* me) and that was It – capital I. Change of plan.

"Him," I said firmly to the owner.

"But you haven't looked at any of the others," she queried.

I did not have to look. Ollie had chosen *me*. He was as poor an excuse for a dog as you could ever see: neglected and abandoned as he had outlived his usefulness. He had undoubtedly been used for rabbit and hare coursing, but at only one year old, he was already slowing down and had been discarded and found wandering the streets; starving, cold and thin as a rake. He was scruffy and tattered, but – *oh!* – ever so desperate to return with me. I asked how old he was and the rescue staff reckoned that he was about one.

"Yep," I said, "he's the one."

And he was.

Ollie was about 18 years old at the time of our move to Gozo and he had been my best friend for 17 of those years. He had been there through some of the toughest times of my life and had certainly saved my sanity when I went through a horrendous divorce. He did that by simply sitting with his wet nose on my lap at the time and occasionally grunting to remind me that he was there. So after *much* deliberation and discussion, it was agreed that the most sensible option in our getting safely to Gozo was to buy a Luton-type lorry, fill it up with all our stuff, make a safe place for Ollie, sleep over in the cab *en route* and there you have it.

Simple, wasn't it? Sigh. To cut a long story short, we scoured the local papers in vain and finally turned to *Ebay,* where we found and bought from Newcastle a 26-foot Luton-type lorry with a hydraulic tail-lift. After many phone calls, photographs and discussions with the owner, Steve went up on the train, drove it, looked it over, agreed the deal and brought it back. I marvelled at the lorry, laughing with excitement at the huge amount of space we suddenly had, to pack up our lives and take it all with us.

Thus began the unenviable task of packing. I quail at the memory of it and a tear forms in the corner of my eye. We agreed that we would sell as much of the big stuff as we could, such as the freezer, fridge, dishwasher and so on, as we were going into a furnished flat which had everything we needed – and, anyway, I certainly did not fancy lugging white goods up three flights of stairs! One slight snag, however, was that I was working away from home at the time, from Monday to Friday, so I was not there to oversee the sale of all those goods. I can almost feel the collective sigh of women the world over at the prospect of leaving the man in charge – especially when said man's mind was almost exclusively focussed on route planning all the way to Gozo and packing his big, new toy of a lorry.

Steve would ring me and say something like, "There's a guy wants the freezer," (advertised for £150 as it was almost brand new and had cost me £350), "he offered us £85 so I sold it."

I would close my eyes and count to 10 before asking, "You did whaaat?! You let it go for HOW MUCH??"

And so on. That was pretty much a daily occurrence and I came to dread the phone ringing.

One Monday morning, I had set off for work at my usual 4.30am – I had to get from Chesterfield to Norwich and there was no motorway. Steve was still oblivious to a new day dawning, so I should have known better than to try to give any instructions. We had more things for sale and I spoke into his ear, very slowly and clearly.

"Try not to sell anything too cheaply. Remember, it's all nearly new," I hissed.

No response. Not even an eye flickered. Later that day, came the phone call.

"Hey, guess what?" Steve said, sounding very pleased with himself. "I sold the cooker."

"Whaaat?!" was my strangled reply.

"I sold the cooker. Good, eh?! And I got a good price for it too," he boasted.

"You sold *my* cooker??" I asked, leaving a silence for the count of three before bursting his bubble. "You sold the cooker, eh, darling? Do you know that it wasn't actually for sale?"

And that is how we got to live on microwaved meals for the next two weeks before we actually moved. Steve, however, was right – he *had* gotten a good price for the cooker. I must note here that despite selling the entire contents of my kitchen, Steve managed to hang on to every one of his 17 guitars, two drum kits, two keyboards, 10 pairs of speakers, six amplifiers and other musical accessories too numerous to mention, but which would about fill the lorry from front to back and top to bottom!

After much standing around and staring, measuring and thinking, the lorry was duly loaded and – I have to admit – it was a beautiful job. Everything had a place and Steve's drilling and hammering skills ensured that nothing – but nothing – would slip, move or fall over. The last thing aboard was his 600cc Suzuki motorbike, which he managed to cram in. The plan was to go and say our goodbyes to family before leaving on our adventure of a road trip. Steve would go first with the lorry and I would follow two days later with Ollie after I had finished work. The day dawned for Steve to set off.

"Well," I said, excitedly, "this is it, the beginning of the journey."

I wished Steve luck and we said goodbye. I turned to old Ollie who was curled up in his basket, ignoring the excitement.

"Just me and you now, matey," I told the dog who condescended to look in my direction as if to say, *I can see that.*

I knew it was too good to last. Just two hours into Steve's trip, disaster struck. The lorry had almost veered off the road, apparently due to the snapping of a leaf spring. Steve had, at least, managed to avoid an accident and nursed the injured lorry to a garage, but he was told that *both* leaf springs were terminally ill. The guy who sold it to us would have undoubtedly known that and it would take £1500 to fix!

As the guy who had sold us that lemon of a vehicle owned a commercial garage and had given us a commercial receipt, I rang him immediately to demand what he intended to do about the whole thing. No prizes here for guessing. The guy denied all responsibility and told me not to bother him again. There then followed days of raging phone calls to *Trading Standards* who eventually paid him a visit. However, the guy spun them a story about the lorry being privately owned, thus exempt from the commercial aspect of it all. And so, despite being warned by *Trading Standards* that they would be keeping an eye on him and his dodgy trading, at the end of the day we were undeniably stuffed.

After weeping with rage for the best part of half a day, I scraped myself up off the floor and started considering plan B, albeit with puffy eyes. The problem, of course, was that we did not actually have plan B – plan A had been *it*. Adding to our problems was the ever-impending bad weather. It was December 2010 and you may recall the atrocious snow and ice which the UK experienced at that time. The snow was threatening and Steve was warning darkly that if we did not set off within the week, we would be stuck in the UK until after New Year's Day. We were, in effect, homeless so that was definitely not an attractive prospect. In addition, we had commitments in Gozo to perform several shows over the Christmas period and did not want to let people down.

Having wasted £2000 of our hard-earned savings on the lorry, we were struggling to come to terms with the prospect of spending another £1500 to fix it. We did not feel we had any other options – apart from the obvious repairs which were needed, the lorry was sound. Then came the decider as, to my horror, I discovered that a lorry had to go through the Channel tunnel as freight – and guess what? Pets were not allowed through in freight vehicles. The words *bad to worse* did not even begin to cover it. We had not even left UK soil, yet our great plans were already unravelling and our savings were disappearing faster than ice in a volcano.

It was, however, an easier decision to agree that we would not spend any more money getting the lorry fixed as we now knew that we could not use it because of Ollie. So with gritted teeth we sold it for £1000 to a project which exported lorry parts to Africa. That was it: our dream was disappearing fast and then there was all the STUFF! I mean, where the hell do you put the entire contents of a house, a 45-foot shed, a lifetime of music equipment, not to mention a jukebox which weighed a ton and a 600cc motorbike? We needed plan B and fast.

We owned a pretty powerful car at the time: a 6-cylinder, 2.6 *Vectra*. It was more than capable of towing a trailer, so what if . . . . . ? Yes, that was it. We would get a tow-bar attached, buy a trailer, transfer the stuff into it and be on our way. Enthused, we managed to find a decent box trailer for £1700 and, after all, we would be able to sell it at the other end. Things were looking up again. One snag, though: contents of a 26-foot Luton lorry into a 2-ton trailer do not go! There followed a frantic race against the weather to decide what *had* to go with us, what could be stored in the UK and what could be given away to charity shops. I cringe at the memory of the perfectly good things we gave away as time ran out and the weather closed in. Steve was, for the most part, in the lorry, literally throwing things out of the side door.

He kept saying, "This can go, this can go, get rid of this," endlessly.

I gave away a brand new microwave – just one of the things I would later bitterly regret having got rid of, not realising at the time just how much those sort of things cost in Gozo. It really came down to the wire as the snow got serious; huge thick flakes and it was sticking. Visibility was rapidly disappearing and soon it would be too late and dangerous to drive.

"Now!" shouted Steve through the howling winds. "We leave now or we stay until this weather clears!"

That was it. The faffing about was over. With Ollie on the backseat as snug as he could be, the trailer hitched, the goodbyes were said and we were finally off.

CHAPTER 6

The weather could not have been worse as we embarked on our new lives. It was snowing a blizzard: that mesmerising, swirling snow that comes at your windscreen in a never-ending kaleidoscope of dancing lace, which makes you blink every few seconds to stay focused. It had been snowing for several hours as we made our way gingerly down towards the Channel tunnel. Conditions for regular driving were truly atrocious, but for towing a trailer with two tons of personal effects inside it was borderline insanity.

Steve, however, was on a mission – you know how men get. He had to conquer those miles; failure was not an option. His face was set and his mouth was a determined line. His eyebrows were furrowed with concentration as he drove on and on into the ever-worsening weather. To add to the problems, it was growing dark. There was no conversation; just silence and snow. An occasional grunt emerged from Ollie in the back seat as if to say, *Hey, don't forget I'm here too*. But other than that, I was lost in my thoughts as every bit of Steve's effort went into keeping us all safe.

Was it the right thing to do? Would the grass be greener in Gozo? Steve and I had already made major changes in our lives. We had left our respective spouses to be together and had gone through bitter, acrimonious divorces. I glanced at Steve and my heart skipped as it always did. I loved him with a passion – no regrets there; my strong, steady, dependable, loving and impossibly handsome man. But Gozo? Was *that* right for us?

As Steve drove through the hypnotic snow, my mind wandered back in time to July 2006. Almost seven months had passed since the day I first met that Elvis guy, aka Steve, and fallen head over heels in love with him. It had been a surreal evening, which ended with my going home feeling unsettled and dissatisfied with my life. Of course, I was being unrealistic: I mean, we were both married and since that initial meeting, we had only met one other time and it had been less than encouraging. I had gone out on New Year's Eve of 2005 to, by pure chance, a place where Steve was performing. My heart had done a backflip as soon as I saw him and every, single feeling I had experienced the first time around came flooding back in force. Oh, God! Steve was so impossibly handsome and charming. But despite my smiling and saying hello, he seemed to ignore me and did not speak or acknowledge me at all. I had no idea about things at the time, but he was deeply unhappy and struggling with his own marriage. Steve told me later that he knew precisely where I was at every moment of that night, but could not trust himself to come and speak to me.

So it was with great surprise that I received a phone call in July 2006, asking me if I would like to perform with Steve in a charity event in September of that year. I was speechless. *Me? Sing professionally?* I agreed, of course, but do not mind admitting that I was utterly terrified at the prospect. My singing experience had, to that date, consisted of the school choir which was light years previously and two wins in karaoke competitions. It was hardly the pedigree of a professional singer, but I was not going to miss out on the opportunity, so a date was set for me to visit Steve's home and discuss the arrangements. My husband was also invited, but in his usual, 'encouraging' way he declined the invitation, pouring scorn on the whole idea of my singing in public.

I arrived at Steve's house in a state of nervous anticipation. I was terrified that my schoolgirl feelings would get the better of me and I have to admit, they did. As I sat in his house, sipping politely on the glass of water I had been offered, I hardly dared look at Steve. His presence was overwhelming and I was relieved when it was agreed that we would go into the music room to practice some songs, along with another friend of his who was also due to perform at the charity event. My relief, however, was short-lived as the music room was smaller than I had imagined and I was now even closer to Steve. I felt sure that unless his friend and himself had suddenly been struck blind, they must have been able to see how I was truly feeling. Resisting the urge to fling myself at Steve and declare my undying love for him, I tried to focus on singing, but it was almost impossible.

"How can you possibly need a coffee? We've only just set off," Steve would argue.

Meanwhile, I would sulk and wish I had a flask. No, Steve was the epitome of self-control and I secretly wondered if he was half camel. Ollie was no help at all in that situation, either.

"Ollie needs a wee," was never part of the battle plan.

Ollie had a bladder of cast iron. He was a Marine among dogs as far as his self-control went. His comfort breaks were entirely weather related. If there was the slightest hint of rain – nay, damp – he would shrug, turn back inside and hold it. And, boy, could he hold it! Even Steve was impressed.

One of my greatest worries in moving to Gozo was not the packing (*a nightmare*) or the cost (*incomprehensible*), or even the prospect of getting lost (*inevitable*). No; what kept me awake at night was Ollie. I had followed the guidelines laid out by the UK's Department for the Environment, Food and Rural Affairs (DEFRA) and its Maltese counterpart, in filling out the acres of forms and fulfilling the requirements to move a dog from the UK to the Maltese Islands. Of course, it was just my luck that the UK and Malta had the strictest guidelines in the world. There was the microchipping and the rabies injection, and the blood test to make sure he had gotten the rabies injection, and the passport, and last but not least – and the cause of all my anxieties – the tick-and-tapeworm treatment. And all of it had to be done within certain timeframes. Ollie was required to be treated for ticks and tapeworms no more than 24 hours and not less than 48 hours prior to setting one single, hairy paw on Maltese soil – or was it the other way around: 48 and 24? Oh, I forget! All I know is it gave me a massive headache. In addition, a vet had to stamp his passport to confirm that the tasks had been undertaken, so we could not just turn up in Malta, on the way to Gozo, and say:

"Oh, yeah. We did that."

There had to be proof.

"Do you realise," I asked Steve who was studying his map, "that this means we will probably have to find a vet in Italy? How am I supposed to do that? I mean, even if I do find a vet, what if we're delayed after he's had his treatment? What then? And how do I know where we'll be? And I can't speak Italian."

Fret, fret; worry, worry. Steve did not even look up from his map.

"Mmmm," he replied.

Thankfully – or, at the time, so I thought – the DEFRA website was a positive mine of information and allowed you to print off the requirements in various languages. I went for all of them: German, Swiss, Italian, French . . . . . well, you know; what with my navigating skills and all. I added that small rainforest's worth of paper to my ever-growing stash of 'important papers' that Steve was not allowed to touch. I continued to worry and imagined a scene in which we reached Malta, only to have a sad-looking official mournfully shake his head at us and turn us back to begin again as I had got it all wrong. Matters had been complicated by the fact that we had been given inaccurate information in the UK, which now meant that Ollie would have to spend his first three weeks in Malta incarcerated in quarantine. It was unavoidable due to timeframes on the rabies blood tests, which we had been told did not need to be done until a certain date – incorrect. I will not bore you with the details, but suffice it to say, I was *not* happy.

As we approached the Channel tunnel, I had my first of many nail-biting moments of panic as I prepared our documents to be checked. I braced myself to be banished back home as things were not in order, but it never happened. We made it past the first hurdle and no one seemed the slightest bit interested in one tatty, old lurcher and less so in any canine passport – or any other documentation, for that matter. We were on the train! Now, before we continue, where's my chocolate?

CHAPTER 7

Having had a horrendous trip down to the Channel tunnel, we emerged at the other side of it in France only 25 minutes later. Exciting! But my excitement was short lived as we were met by even worse weather conditions than the ones we had just left behind. The roads were packed solid with several inches of ice and the snow continued falling relentlessly. Perfect! Not only were we now towing a two-ton trailer on packed ice. We were towing with an automatic transmission, on the wrong side of the road, in the dark. All that was not the worst of it, though. The famously unreliable *Satnav*, which I so naively expected to take us all the way to Gozo, did not actually work in Europe. *Non!* Naturally, that immediately became my fault.

"How could you not know this?" asked Steve in a voice usually reserved for small children and the feeble minded.

"How could I know what I don't know?" I argued, futilely.

As I spoke, my stomach cramped and my peanut bladder signalled the need for an immediate, urgent stop as the enormity of the consequences hit me. I was going to have to navigate the whole way. That was bad. It was very, very bad for several reasons:

a) I would get no sleep and I liked to sleep in the car. I enjoyed putting my seat back, snoozing for hours, then waking and saying, "Wow, *that* didn't take long," as Steve hunched gritty-eyed at the wheel;

b) We would now get lost. It was a foregone conclusion, a sad inevitability and I ground my teeth in advance distress, panicking as I imagined Steve trying to reverse and turn the trailer around on some tiny, French, back lane on ice in the dark;

c) I would not be able to switch off and sit eating my way through the cornucopia of a picnic I had prepared.

No. It was highly inconvenient and I suspected that she – the *Satnav* – had done it on purpose. Had I not already identified her as lazy? Well, thank you very much, *Satnav*! I rest my case. Now, it was all down to me and the enormity of the responsibility threatened to crush me.

Steve, like many men, did not suffer poor directions gladly so, great! I had to navigate on ice, in the dark, with all the road signs in a foreign language and I just knew that an hourly toilet break would be out of the question. I looked around wildly in the vain hope that we might find a *Satnav* shop, which was about as realistic a hope as a Bigfoot passing by.

"Which way? Which way?" said Steve with all the patience of an angry wasp.

"Hang on, give me a chance!" I complained as I stalled for time, struggling to find the right page.

It was one of those unnecessarily gargantuan maps of Europe.

"Why's this map so big?" I crabbed, petulantly.

Instantly, I managed to tear the page I needed. *Oh, marvellous!* Now, I had to try and make out the teeny, tiny road numbers and motorway exits along the rip! Thank goodness, I had the foresight to bring along a magnifying glass: not just a magnifying glass, but a light-up magnifying glass. I knew it would prove to be a boon. I squinted along the rip.

"That way," I declared and pointed without any real conviction.

And that was it, we were off.

Steve's need for mile conquering – sorry, we were in Europe now – his need for kilometre conquering took on a new focus. There was absolutely no stopping him, but as we could only go about 35 mph tops given the conditions, I kind of understood from where he was coming. I was, however, extremely grateful for the zillions of gallons of fuel the car was burning by towing in such challenging circumstances. We watched in horror as the fuel gauge literally dropped before our eyes as it ate up the fuel, tank after expensive tank. Nevertheless, it meant that I got to take multiple comfort breaks and keep the peanut happy. On the other hand, Ollie could not be persuaded out of the car in the -15 degree temperature. I would open his door and try sounding enthusiastic:

"C'mon, Ollie, here we go. Let's go for a walk."

The dog would sniff the air with disdain as I stood there, freezing. He would begrudgingly accept a drink, then curl up again into a neat ball on the back seat, ignoring me. I swear I could feel his canine disapproval at my weak bladder.

Steve basically drove non-stop for 24 hours. Yes, we stopped for fuel and I would rush to the *Ladies*, then grab a sandwich and coffee, and we would eat as we drove. Steve never stopped to rest or stretch his legs properly and I am not actually sure he ever went to the loo. Steve and Ollie seemed to just simply reabsorb it all. Finally, Steve showed signs of faltering and I pleaded with him to stop and rest.

We had got as far as Basel in Switzerland; it was a drive of which to be proud. Steve had done it safely and without ceremony, but he was utterly exhausted by the intense concentration it had required. I had congratulated him at regular intervals along the way. As we drove through the pretty villages, I spotted a small hotel.

"There," I shouted and pointed. "Let's stop there."

Steve did not need asking twice. He pulled the car and the trailer over onto a sheet of ice and suggested that I go in and see if they had a room available, before he attempted to park for the night. I had a small moment of panic.

"What if they won't let Ollie in? We can't leave him in the car, he'll freeze to death."

"I'm sure they'll let Ollie in," Steve reasoned.

"But what if they don't? What will we do?" I pressed.

"Well," he continued in a measured tone, "if you'd go in and ask, instead of standing there in the cold, you'd find out."

"Yes, good idea. I'll do that."

It was not an issue and after Steve managed to park the car and the trailer (brilliantly, I might add and with more praise and congratulations from myself), we were welcomed into the family-run hotel and given a meal and a hot drink. We were also given food and a bowl of water for Ollie.

"There is no charge for your lovely dog," said the lady with a smile.

In my emotionally exhausted state, I wanted to cry at that small kindness. Ollie finally admitted to himself that he needed to go out and we pottered around on the ice, skidding and sliding as he made his important decision of the day. Then, to bed. But before we finally fell into blissful unconsciousness, Steve turned to me with a tired smile.

"Well done, sweetheart. You did great," he said.

I fell asleep grinning with delight. I had got us to Basel and to the hotel without as much as one wrong turn. We all slept for a solid 14 hours. Ollie curled up in his usual neat ball on a blanket, dreaming of chasing rabbits in the green fields he had left behind.

We awoke to a bright and beautiful day, but it was still -10 degrees outside and we had an awfully long way to go. Steve went out with Ollie on a boy trip to survey the trailer and declared that it had frozen to the floor! After a great breakfast and many trips to the *Ladies* in anticipation of another marathon drive, we were off again . . . . . well, we were off after rocking the trailer back and forth to liberate it from the ice.

Having got us to Basel without getting lost, my confidence in my navigating skills was at an all-time high. I was even off the ripped page and could see properly where we were meant to be going. Despite having left the UK, crossed France and entered into Switzerland, no one had as yet checked our passports at any border/toll point, never mind asked for Ollie's documents, about which I had fretted so long and hard. All that, however, was about to change. As we approached the Italian border, two stern-looking, uniformed officers indicated that we had to pull over. True to form, I fretted.

"This is it. Oh, God! His papers won't be right and he's not had the tick-and-tapeworm treatment yet," I warbled. "I can't speak any Italian. How will I explain all this to them?" I continued to lament.

"Will you stop fretting?" said Steve, wearily. "It'll be fine."

We got out of the car, leaving Ollie curled up on the back seat. I was hoping that they would not see him.

"What's in the back of the trailer?" asked the officer in perfect English.

"It's all household stuff," answered Steve, pleasantly.

"Open it, please," came the stern reply.

Now, you must remember that we had driven through the Alps and while it had been a stunningly beautiful drive, it had also been, well, pretty hilly. Consequently, all our stuff had shifted considerably. As Steve started lifting the back of the trailer, most of the two tons of contents made a dash for freedom.

"Leave it! Leave it!" spluttered the officer, hastily.

He realised, almost too late, that he was in danger of being buried under a mountain of our belongings.

After a brief discussion as to where we were going and why, and a cursory glance at our passports, we were waved on with wishes of good luck in our new lives. Ollie? They never even asked. We had made it over another hurdle. We were getting there, but we were not there yet.

We gradually left the long, wide, dual carriageways and motorways behind and entered into more built up areas. It was tricky and I needed all my wits about me to concentrate and navigate well, when all I wanted to do was stare out the windows at all the new sights and places. I was so excited I wished that we could have stopped to explore a little more, but it was hardly practical. I mean, you cannot exactly pull into your regular pay-and-display with the rig we had. In addition, we had already been warned darkly by several people that we should *not*, under any circumstances, stop in Italy because "they" – *Who the hell are "they?"* I would like to know – yes, *they* would steal the trailer and all its contents. That, of course, sparked a fresh outburst from me.

"What? Well, that's great! We go all that way to be mugged for all our worldly goods. Well, that's typical. It *would* happen to us, wouldn't it?"

Steve gave me *that* look and said, "Nothing's happened and nothing's going to happen, okay?"

But just to be sure, we nipped and bought a wheel clamp . . . . . well, you never knew.

The ice and snow were behind us now and had given way to torrential rain and high winds. There was zero chance of Ollie getting out of the car in that weather. He huddled closer into the seat and made himself invisible. As we drove into Genova, we reached an unexpected conclusion: it was costing us an alarming amount of savings to continue driving all the way down to Malta. We still had to go all across Italy and, to be honest, neither of us had the stomach for it. We were also getting concerned at the impact on Ollie of having to be in the backseat for hours on end – not that he seemed to mind or care. He had regular access to water and lots of food and treats, and it seemed that he was doing the best of us all.

At the end, having counted our dwindling savings, we agreed that we would instead take the Genova ferry. It would sail for 24 hours to Palermo and we could book a dog cabin so that Ollie could be with us. We would have a real bed. Furthermore, it would be more comfortable than sleeping in the car – a real possibility as we really did not want to leave the trailer unattended, just in case the mysterious *they* stole it.

Decision made, we began searching for a hotel. It was not a small task in an unknown city, with the rain lashing down and a car and a trailer to park safely. At the back of my mind also lurked the ever-growing worry about Ollie getting his tick-and-tapeworm treatment. Once I had booked us onto the ferry, there was no going back. He *had* to get the treatment as soon as possible or we could really be refused entry with him into Malta. After driving in circles around Genova, Steve finally managed to find a parking space on the road. It was, however, a parking meter. We could not read the instructions which were in Italian, but I had some euros so I stuffed a handful of them into the machine, hoping it would be enough. Then we put the ticket in the front window and headed off to the *Holiday Inn* which we could see beckoning to us 200 yards away. Little did I realise that when I slammed the car door shut, the wind had whipped the parking ticket off the dashboard and onto the floor, out of sight.

With Ollie in tow, we made a rain-soaked dash to the hotel and asked if they spoke English. Of course, they did and yes, they had a room and, even better, Ollie was welcome. *Woohoo, bliss!* We were to have two nights as there was no ferry the following day. Finally, Steve could rest and recharge his batteries, and I could indulge in a nice, hot bath. We now needed to find what all of us, including Ollie, were craving: *McDonalds!* Oh, yum, there was one across the street. Having survived on cold, service station sandwiches and crisps for the last few days, we ordered a ridiculous amount of salty junk and sat happily munching. Ollie gave us his best, fixed lurcher stare and we did not leave him out. He got his own chicken nuggets and burger – and at almost 19 years old, why not!

Once again, we had a blissful night's sleep, but I knew that the following day I simply *had* to tackle the dreaded tick-and-tapeworm issue. So out came the DEFRA paperwork which I had carefully printed in Italian – and in three other languages, just in case. I handed it to the desk staff and they nodded, picked up the phone and rang a local vet, explained to him what we needed and called us a taxi to take us there. Talk about service! We got to the vet's where he read the paperwork and nodded. I had brought the tick-and-tapeworm treatment with me in case we could not find it on our travels, so all he had to do was administer it to Ollie and sign the passport to say that it was done.

Ollie stood patiently, without any fuss, and allowed that total stranger to prod and poke at him. The vet could not believe us when we told him Ollie's age. He waved his arms in dramatic astonishment and fussed over our lurcher with love and biscuits. Ollie lapped it all up and I sighed in immense relief. It was done. The one thing I had so fretted about was done! We just had to get to Malta in less than 48 hours – or else it would have to be done again. *No pressure there, then.* The vet waved away our enquiries as to how much we owed him. He shook his head and made it clear even with a language barrier that he wanted no payment. We left him with 20 euros and our grateful thanks. We were good to go.

CHAPTER 8

D ue to the startlingly high cost of fuel to tow the trailer in such dreadful weather, bankruptcy was looking increasingly likely if we continued our journey by car. In light of that, we had decided to travel the next leg of the journey by ferry from Genova to Palermo. It was going to be a restful, 24-hour sailing with the added luxury of a cabin, so that Ollie could be with us and we would have a bed for the night.

I had rung up the ferry company prior to beginning our trip as we had initially considered it an option. We had originally been quoted 250 euros for the trip and had – foolishly, as it turned out – thought that driving would be cheaper. Naturally, that quote had been weeks ago and I now stood in front of the ticket booth in Genova asking for passage the very next day.

"500 euros?!" I spluttered. "But I rang a few weeks ago and it was only 250!"

The man shrugged his shoulders and could not have looked less interested. *Sigh.* We had no choice. Actually, that is not precisely true; we did have a choice: either pay it or drive. And we knew that it was going to cost us a lot more than 500 euros in fuel to drive across Italy in a car, with automatic transmission, towing a two-ton load. We had already spent in excess of 1000 euros in petrol – yes, 1000 euros, to get that far. So I bought us the tickets.

We were on the move again. We packed up our things and went to retrieve the car which, you will recall, we had parked on a side street, complete with the required parking ticket from the meter. Unfortunately, neither of us had realised that the wind had blown the ticket off the dashboard as I slammed shut the door of the car. Yep, we had a parking ticket all right! It was in Italian and we did not understand a word. What were the chances of us being traced? We considered our options, looked at each other in complete accord, screwed it up and left.

The queue for the Genova ferry had not yet begun to form, so we were first in line. With an occasional, nervous glance over my shoulder for the traffic warden, whom I expected to see bearing down on us shouting in Italian because of the parking ticket, we were pretty settled. We found a little café which did more than acceptable snacks, although at a price. As we waited, we were thrilled to see Michael Schumacher's *Formula 1* truck pull in right beside us. As avid fans, that was a rare treat. Ollie, however, was unimpressed. We made it onto the ferry without any problems and, to our delight, discovered that Ollie had been given a doggy bag of beef jerky treats, courtesy of *Virtu Ferries*. NOW he was impressed. We had no idea, however, of the mayhem those innocuous beef jerkies would cause. Oh, if only we had known!

The dog cabins on the ferry were sensibly situated on a separate deck of their own, allowing the owners to take their dogs outside onto the deck to do what they needed to do. There were hosepipes, shovels and all manner of helpful accessories to ensure the decks were kept clean and tidy. I took Ollie onto the deck and he stood there, blinking like an old sea dog as he enjoyed the breeze and swaying slightly to keep himself balanced. He wandered around on the deck, but could not be persuaded to use it as a toilet. Ollie was not accustomed to relieving himself on wooden decking, so he politely, but pointedly, refused to go. Having huge confidence in Ollie's cast iron bladder and overall control of himself, I was not too worried. He would let me know when he needed to go, I figured. Off we went back to the cabin. Night, night.

We settled down to sleep with Steve and myself in the cabin's two single beds, and Ollie on a blanket on the lino – *thank God!* – floor.

"Watch that shelf above your head," Steve warned as we got into our individual, tiny beds.

I was drifting off into peaceful slumber when I was brought fully awake by the unmistakeable sound of a lurcher having a toilet emergency. It was dark and anxious as I was to hurry him outside, I leapt out of bed. Now, for those of you with a weak constitution, I suggest you discontinue reading at this point. It was not good; not good at all.

Ollie's overindulgence on the beef jerkies – *thank you VERY much, Virtu Ferries!* – had an extremely unfortunate effect on his normally robust digestive system. He had, in short, got the squits! Remember, I had jumped out of bed? Yes, you are absolutely correct in what you are thinking. I leapt straight into a squishy liquid mass of lurcher poo, resembling a small pond. I slipped, skidded and realised with incoherent horror what was unfolding.

"No, no! Oh, God! Ollie! No, mate!" I yelled without effect.

Ollie's usual control of steel had deserted him as he hunched and strained to get rid of the dratted treats which were causing him such distress.

"Steve! Steve, wake up!" I shouted with my feet covered in sticky, treacly poo. "Oh, God!" I repeated, "Oh, good God; it's everywhere!"

Steve came to in what I call his SAS fighting mode.

"What? What's happening?" he yelled, sitting bolt upright and banging his head on the low shelf.

"Ollie's pooing everywhere," I wailed, "and I've stood in it. Put the light on," I pleaded.

I think I preferred it in the dark. The scene with lights on was definitely worse than I could have imagined. Ollie was still on a roll, pumping poo out like some sort of jammed cement mixer. There was no stopping it. I *had* to get him outside as the cabin was filling up and the smell was indescribable. I gagged. I had never been good with poo or sick, but this, *this* was like a nightmare. I skidded to the bathroom, shoved my sticky feet under the shower and got the worse of it off. I grabbed Ollie's lead, somehow got it on and waited for a lull in what had become a fascinating, but horrific, production line of poo. Finally, Ollie stopped and looked mightily relieved with himself.

"Now," yelled Steve. "Go, now!"

He was still in SAS mode, but I did not need to be told twice. I opened the cabin door and set off the 20 yards to the deck. It was not far, 20 yards, but it may well have been the length of an entire football field. I seemed to be moving in slow motion – no pun intended.

"Come on, mate. Come on," I chivvied the lurcher. "Quickly, now," as Ollie strolled along as though we were on a Sunday school outing.

Then it happened. Ollie stopped.

"Oh, no! No, no, no, no, no!" I wailed. "Not now! Oh, please! Not now, Ollie; not here!"

Too late. His bowels began to spasm and the lurcher *had* to go – he absolutely had to go *now*, right there and then on the nice carpet. Ollie hunched and strained and there it came. *Oh, God!* It was worse than before; even the lurcher looked startled. There was nothing else for it. I dragged Ollie unceremoniously out onto the deck, leaving a trail of evil, smelling, chocolatey liquid behind us like a giant snail trail. Once on the deck, I abandoned Ollie to his fate, knowing there was nowhere else he could go. He was safe out there. I ran as fast as I could back to the cabin where Steve was gamely trying to clean up the lake of poo in there. I was crying; really crying.

"He's poo'd all over the corridor," I gasped. "Help me! Oh, please come and help me! We *have* to clean the mess before anyone sees it."

And there it was, our disaster aboard the *Virtu* ferry. Naturally, now we laugh about it all. In fact, we laughed even the very next day. But at the time . . . . . oh, at the time, it was *not* funny at all. Poor old Ollie! He recovered remarkably quickly and even had the cheek to snuffle around looking for more treats. The carpet was never quite the same afterwards and the next day, I walked stealthily along, taking furtive glances to see if there were any hidden video cameras that might have recorded the whole, shameful incident. There were none, although the brown stain on the carpet acted like a beacon. It might as well have been lit up and flashed. I knew it was there and could not get off that ferry fast enough.

The rest of the trip passed without further incident, to our relief. Ollie was back to normal. He even managed to lower his standards and use the deck for the purpose it was intended. We arrived safe and sound in Palermo the next day and we were ready to go. Sicily, there we were.

The ferries crossing between Malta and Gozo

Chapter 9

Having slunk off the ferry praying that no one would identify us as the owners of the dog who had emptied his bowels all over their nice red carpet, we were once again on the road. The weather was improving all the time and the ice and snow were distant memories. The ferry incident, however, was still horrifyingly fresh in my mind and I wanted us to put as much distance between Palermo and ourselves as possible, as quickly as we could.

Now, at the risk of waking up with the head of a horse in my bed, for the record I would like to say that the standard of driving in Sicily is probably the worst we have ever witnessed – and having driven through most of Europe and not a little of the United States in our time, we speak from considerable experience. It was a nightmare from the moment we disembarked. Cars would literally fly at us from side streets when it was clearly our right of way. That did nothing to deter them. They, no doubt, spied a slow moving car and trailer, and thought they would quickly get in front of us. Add to that the maniacal, overtaking manoeuvres which threatened to force us off the road and you get some idea of how it was. Steve had driven tanks in the Army and the macho young men soon realised that they had more than met their match as he went once again into SAS mode.

"Eh? Eh? Come on, then! Doesn't matter to me, mate," Steve declared, menacingly. "I'll hit you with this thing," he continued with his own, older and wiser, macho bravado.

Silently, I clung to the car door, my bladder shrieking internally for respite. I imagined Steve using the trailer as a battering ram and knew that he was more than capable of it if pushed too far. Words were futile. A man driving under threat does not want to hear:

"Calm down," much less, "Ooh, look, there's a quaint little café. Why don't we pull over for a nice coffee?"

His blood is up and he just wants to be at the front of the queue.

Amazingly, apart from the below baseline driving standards, we made it across Sicily in one piece with remarkably little drama and arrived many hours later at the tiny port of Pozzallo. That was easier said than done as there were precious few signs indicating where the port might be and, of course, all the road signs were in Italian. But we made it, eventually. We were mighty pleased to discover that we were first in the queue for the fast catamaran that would whisk us over to Valletta, Malta in under 90 minutes. We were lucky in meeting some other English people who had made the trip before. They advised us that the ferry would not be there for many hours yet, but there was a small snack bar over the way, which is where we all headed. Coffee was most definitely required.

We drank expensive coffee at tourist prices and slept fitfully in the car. Ollie, glad of the warmth, deigned to go for a few short walks, sniffing and exploring the new, unfamiliar environment with little enthusiasm. I waited anxiously for the ticket office to open, which it ultimately did and tickets were purchased without further ado. We led the queue onto the ferry knowing that Ollie could not join us on the deck, but had to remain in the car. That made me nervous. We had not left him alone for the entire trip and I was apprehensive as to how he would react. We left the lurcher with water and a bowl of his favourite dried food, patted his head and said goodbye with reassurances that we would return soon. Ollie surveyed us with an all-knowing eye, curled up into his famous ball and closed his eyes. I need not have worried.

In the surprisingly luxurious lounge upstairs, I explained to a member of the staff that I had a very old dog in the car. He kindly agreed to my going down at regular intervals to make sure that the dog was okay – as a rule, passengers are not allowed down onto the car deck once the catamaran has sailed. Each time I went down, Ollie was curled up fast asleep and remained that way for the duration of the sailing. The old sea dog was a better traveller than most people.

Finally, we came within sight of the beautiful, ancient port of Valletta, Malta. The catamaran made its way slowly and carefully into the dock and that was it; we were there! I tried to take it all in at once. The history of the place was legendary and to be standing on the deck of a boat as it sailed majestically into port was a real thrill. We were surrounded by tall stone buildings with breathtakingly beautiful architecture. You could almost hear the marching, ghostly footsteps of the Knights of the Order of Saint John making their way through the cobbled streets.

My excitement was at an all-time high, but tinged with some stress as now we had to contact a local vet and get Ollie to quarantine. We would not be permitted to leave the dock with the lurcher, so we were once again on unfamiliar territory in an unknown situation. Once we disembarked, we set foot on Maltese soil for the first time as residents. It felt good and warm, despite only being December. Ollie woke up and tottered around, once again taking it all in and accepting a fuss from the port officials who immediately fell for his tattered charm. We were given a phone number for the vet who, when spoken to, assured us that he would be with us in 10 minutes.

It was our first lesson in GMT: not Greenwich Mean Time, but Gozo Maybe Time. If anyone in Malta or Gozo gives you a time, you can pretty much double it and then some! It is an entirely laid-back culture. There is no rush; everything can wait. Well, we waited, we waited and we waited. Ollie paced; we paced. We rang again.

"Yes, yes, I'm close by," lied the vet.

The minutes kept on ticking by.

"This is silly now," I complained to Steve.

To be honest, had we not been so open in saying that we had Ollie with us, we could, no doubt, have driven straight to Gozo and no one would have been any the wiser. Not that I am, for one minute, suggesting that anyone try this, neither am I condoning bringing an animal into a foreign country without the proper precautions. But, just saying, we could have!

Finally, the vet arrived – two hours after we had arrived. He was a friendly, affable man who immediately took to Ollie and made a big fuss of him, which Ollie accepted as his divine right in life. We followed the vet to the quarantine kennels 10 minutes away and on arrival, Ollie was checked over. For the first time during the entire trip, his papers and documents were inspected. Everything was, thankfully, in order. We would not be turned back as I had feared. Ollie was then shown to the kennel which would be his home for the next three weeks. He was allowed to have his own comfortable bed and as many treats and goodies from us as we liked. We could visit him whenever we wanted and were assured that he would be in good hands. No one could believe how old he was and exclamations of amazement were made all around.

With great reluctance, we left Ollie there. He was not too impressed with that unorthodox move. It had not been on his agenda and he stood staring after us as we left him. Ollie was not a dog who barked or even whined, but on that occasion he did. He whined so loudly, poor thing, that we could hear it ringing in our ears as we drove away. I was in tears. Ollie, no doubt satisfied that he had laid enough guilt on us, would end up lying down and falling asleep the moment we were out of sight.

We then had to negotiate our way to the Gozo ferry. The route was well signed and the short trip passed without incident. I drank in the sights and sounds of Malta, marvelling at the history, the rocky shoreline, the clear blue seas, the ancient towering monuments we saw dotted about and the newness of the whole atmosphere. But the notorious Maltese roads were something else! There were potholes all over the place and the whole experience was, in general, bumpy and uncomfortable. We eventually made it to the ferry and were directed into a queue where we sat in anticipation of what was next.

The 25-minute ferry ride was one of the most glorious things I had ever experienced. We wanted to make the most of the warm December weather, so we went up onto the deck to enjoy the spectacular views of Malta, Gozo and Comino; all visible from that one vantage point. I loved it and drank it all in, repeating to myself over and over, like a train on a track:

"We live here, we live here!"

I leaned on the railings and tried to capture the moment forever in my heart. As the ferry sailed smoothly on, I glanced at Steve and saw that he too was almost in a trance as he took it all in. How far we had come – and not just in terms of geography! With the hypnotic hum of the ship's engines in my ears, I allowed my mind to wander freely once again as I reminded myself of just *how* far we had come.

~ ~ ~ ~ ~

I drifted back in memory to September 2006, to a time when I had felt like I was the first and only woman in the world to be secretly in love. My days were consumed thinking about Steve and the impending charity event which was to be my debut as a professional singer. I was distracted at work and at home. I could not focus on anything and lost weight faster than any diet ever invented. I had continued visiting Steve's house for rehearsals and after two visits, began picking up vibes from him which indicated that he might – just might – be feeling the same way. Never in my life having embarked on an affair, I was absolutely terrified and still could not shake off the feeling that everyone around me could read my mind and knew what I was thinking. I think it is called guilt.

The final practice was over and the show was in two days. As I left his house that night, Steve said that he would give me his mobile number in case I needed to ask him anything. Unbeknown to me, Steve never gave anyone his personal mobile number. He explained that as I was so new to singing, I might need to ask something prior to the show or have last minute nerves. His wife eyed him suspiciously and pointedly said that I could ring the house number, but the deed was done. I had his number and saw the secret smile in his eyes as I left the house that night.

The following morning, as I was on my way to work, I received a text message. Now, for most people, this is a common part of any day and they probably receive dozens of text messages. But me? I rarely got any. My husband at the time had never sent me a text, so it was only if one of my daughters wanted to contact me that I would get one. As it was 8.30am, I reckoned that it was not one of the girls. With my heart pounding and my hands trembling, I pulled over to read it, hoping against hope . . . . . there it was, a text from Steve. It simply said:

> *How are you today? I couldn't sleep last night and I don't know why as I never get nervous before a show.*

That was it. I hugged the phone to my chest, reading a million things into that text. After agonising for many minutes, I texted back saying:

> *Me too, I'm not sleeping either, but I think I know why.*

And so it began. A simple, innocuous text in a layby and my world would never be the same again.

The day of the show finally arrived and I had taken a day off from work. Steve had agreed to meet me at the venue, so that I could practice some more as I was really nervous. When he walked in, I was on such a high and felt a happiness that I had not felt in many years. I ran over to Steve, put my arms around him in what I hoped was an acceptable and friendly hug, while breathing in his delicious aftershave.

"Hello, Elvis," I said.

Thus it began. The rest of that day passed in an atmosphere of electricity as we both threw out signals to test the water. By the end of the evening, there was no doubt left in either of our minds. We were in love. How we would work that out, we had no idea and we knew that we would hurt people, but love really *is* blind. It is also completely selfish, but sometimes you just have to reach out and grab a chance for happiness when it is offered. Affairs do not just happen. There is a jumping off point, a decision, which has to be made – and it takes two to tango.

I recall that my husband at the time attended the show. He had not wanted to do so, but had been shamed into supporting me by our daughter. He had sat looking positively disinterested throughout and at the end, when I went down into the audience, he half-heartedly handed me some flowers. I looked at them pointedly and knew without a shred of doubt that my 'friend'– I use the word advisedly here – had actually bought them and given them to him, to give to me. My husband had not bought me flowers in years and as I regarded them, a kind of devil-may-care madness came over me.

"Why are you pretending to have bought me flowers?" I declared.

There was an awkward silence as the surrounding company absorbed this hand grenade of a question. The friend stepped forward and nervously said:

"Oh, no; no. He did buy them for you." Then she added, "Didn't you?" while glaring at my husband in a very pointed manner.

I ignored her and the flowers.

"No, he didn't," I replied. "And I don't know why you're all pretending he did. He didn't even want to be here, so save it."

And I walked off, leaving the entire group open-mouthed.

I had never felt more empowered: me, the stereotypical doormat of a wife had finally given back some of what I had been getting for years. I felt chains falling off as I walked back to the dressing room. I also felt clear-headed and free. Whatever was, or was not, going to happen between Steve and myself, I knew that I would not remain in that loveless sham of a relationship with that miserable, mean-spirited man. I stepped back into the dressing room grinning from ear to ear. My grin transformed into jaw-dropping shock as I picked up my phone and found a message from Steve:

Will you be my girlfriend?

My eyes blurred as my world tilted and my head swam. That was it; it was really happening. I took a deep breath and made the biggest decision of my life. Summoning all my courage, I walked to the edge of the deck and jumped ship. As I fell, I felt like *Alice in Wonderland* falling down the rabbit hole into an unknown world. It was a gut-swooping, wonderful fall. I was finally off the sinking vessel and just in time: just when I had thought that I would hit the water and drown, the lifeboat who was Steve caught me.

~ ~ ~ ~ ~

Meanwhile, the bump of the ferry as it pulled alongside the dock brought me back once again to the present. The afternoon December air was warm and balmy as we made our way on the final leg of what had been a journey of over 1700 miles. Gozo seemed pleasantly familiar to us, having had two holidays there. Steve negotiated the last few miles in the grateful knowledge that his epic drive was almost over. The mutual feeling was surreal. We had done it; we had finally arrived in Gozo. We were home!

The question now was: Would the grass be greener?

CHAPTER 10

Ollie

With Ollie safe and sound in quarantine, we were free to settle into our first flat in Gozo. The flat we had planned to have for a few months was occupied for the first week upon our arrival, so we had to have a temporary one for that time period. Both flats were practically next door to each other in the seaside village of Marsalforn, with its fantastic promenade, complete with numerous cafés and restaurants. We would have no shortage of places to visit.

Thankfully, garages in Gozo are often cavernous. It is not unusual for a family to store three or four cars in them, along with masses of other belongings. Steve easily managed to back the car and the trailer into the garage underneath the flat, off the road and out of the way in that way only men do – looking over his shoulder, one hand on the passenger seat headrest, one on the steering wheel and *Whoosh!* it was parked. Sorry, ladies, I do not care what anyone says. We cannot compete.

Then came the backbreaking work of carrying everything up three flights of stairs into an equally huge flat. We had to be selective as we were only in that flat for a week, so we just took up the clothes and the basics. It was no small task as everything had shifted in the trailer and stuff was quite difficult to locate. Even though it had been less than a week since we packed it, we had no idea what was in the numerous flight cases we had for the trip. It was hit and miss as we opened this case and that case, exclaiming in excitement as if we had been deprived of our things for years on end.

"Oh, I love these shoes," I uttered in delight, hugging them to myself with the memory of a goldfish, having forgotten that I had got them with me.

Steve was equally delighted to be reunited with tools and 'man stuff.' I could see him mentally making space for them wherever we eventually lived. A 'man drawer' was going to be inevitable.

Exhausted after repeatedly running up and down three flights of stairs, we decided that an outing was in order. We wandered down into Marsalforn and had a well-earned drink at a local bar. The evening was warm and, oh, so quiet as it was out of season. We reflected on the last few days; so much had happened. We had travelled so far – about 1700 miles in all – but we were in Gozo and it felt so right. I could not shake the wonderful feeling that we were not on holiday and did not have to go home. We lived there now and I was struggling to get my head around the newness of that concept.

I kept repeating to Steve, "We live here, we live abroad!" while grinning with delight.

The week passed by quickly. We rang the kennels every day and were assured that Ollie was fine, but on day three we decided to head for Malta to visit him. We once again made that marvellous, scenic trip across the three-mile stretch of water to Malta. I never grew tired of that journey. I have even been known to ride the ferry back and forth like a mini-cruise, just to admire the view and enjoy the warm sun and the sea.

We arrived at the kennels and explained that we were there to see Ollie, anxiously asking if he had been okay. The staff looked at us, puzzled.

"Ollie?" they asked, looking blank.

I felt panic. *Oh, no! They lost him,* I thought, *and they did not even know who he was!* Not good at all.

"Yes, Ollie," I repeated. "Scruffy lurcher, about yay big, came in three days ago."

A light dawned in one of the men's eyes. They lit up and creased at the corners with delight as this man realised about whom I was talking.

"Ahh," he exclaimed in recognition. *"Bużnannu!"*

"Sorry?" I asked. "Who?"

There then followed a loud discussion among the all-male staff. There was laughing and smiling all around and we felt as if we were being excluded from the funniest joke ever told. I looked at Steve; he shrugged his shoulders and looked bemused. The manager stepped forward, towards us. He had clearly been elected to explain to us what they were laughing about. He cleared his throat and started:

"Bużnannu!" he repeated, importantly. *"Bużnannu* means great-grandfather in Maltese."

Suddenly, it all made sense. The staff were so taken with Ollie and his age that they had nicknamed him *Bużnannu* – the great-grandfather. We laughed in relief and were pleased that Ollie had found a place in their hearts.

We were led through to the compound where Ollie (or *Bużż* as he was now forever to be nicknamed by ourselves) was wandering around free. The manager explained that everyone loved him so much that they let him have more free time than any other dog as he was so well behaved. On seeing us, Ollie went, quite simply, bananas.

As a rule, Ollie was not a dog given to enthusiasm of any sort. Like Steve, the lurcher's best effort of pleasure usually extended to perhaps a raised eyebrow. He was not given to unnecessary, dramatic shows of emotion or affection, but that day he sure put on a show for us. Ollie raced up and down the compound, his speed defying his 19 years.

"Slow down, you old fool," I shouted in delight. "You'll do yourself a mischief."

But Ollie was not finished. He charged round and round, showing off as he did 'funny runs' – where a dog tucks his tail underneath his body, lowers the undercarriage and charges as fast as he can (owners of lurchers will know exactly what I mean). He was like a cartoon, but at almost 19 years old, his energy was soon spent and he stood panting with the effort of displaying his pleasure. It was reciprocal and while I did not quite rush up and down the compound similarly doing funny runs, we hugged and fussed over Ollie for the longest time. The dog, naturally, looked for food – and he was not disappointed. We were able to give him his favourite treats. The staff told us that Ollie had become the kennel favourite in no time. They competed among themselves to be the one to care for him and always allowed him out as soon as possible. Our lurcher was, in short, ruined. We were delighted and felt reassured that he was in such good hands.

The visit went by too fast, but Ollie was not *that* upset to be left again. After all, he had a family of new friends there to fuss over him. On subsequent visits, we were able to observe Ollie display similar delight in seeing one of the staff. He had not seen us arrive and it was wonderful to see him so happy, greeting the staff with such obvious pleasure. The dog thrived in quarantine. The care he received was second to none and his time there went by quickly.

Then the day arrived for us to take our lurcher back home. Ollie seemed to know that it was time to leave. He actually barked when we arrived and we stared at each other in astonishment.

"He barked!" I said in wonder.

"He knows," replied Steve.

And Ollie did. For the first time in three weeks, he made an immediate dash for the gate. He could not get out fast enough and after *a lot* of attention and fuss from the staff, we repeated our heartfelt thanks, said our goodbyes and set off for home – with *Bużnannu* once again curled up in that ball on his familiar backseat.

We had been worried about the amount of steps Ollie had to go up, to reach the flat – needlessly as it turned out. He bounded up the stairs two at a time, dragging me behind him, eager to explore his new home. We had bought him a new bed, complete with fleecy blanket. He went straight to it, did a few circles, a fair bit of digging to arrange it to his particular taste and that was it: he was home. Ollie soon got the hang of nipping up and down the stairs to go for a walk and, with his cast iron control, two walks a day were sufficient for him.

One day after his walk, I allowed Ollie off his lead to climb the stairs. I usually kept him on a lead, but thought *Well, where can he go? It is up, up and up. What can go wrong?* Little did I know! On that particular day, the man in the flat opposite to us, who usually resided in Malta, had arrived to stay for the weekend. He was home, cooking something that smelled delicious – and his front door was open in what any self-respecting, greedy lurcher would interpret as an invitation to dinner. Ollie raced up the stairs and straight into that man's flat, accepting the 'welcome' with a grin. I followed in hot pursuit.

"Ollie, no!" I called out, feebly.

No effect. I reached the top of the stairs, mentally noting that I needed to work out and get fit as my 19-year-old dog was outrunning me.

"Ollie!" I repeated more firmly. "Come here, now!"

Ollie did not come. Instead, a rather startled-looking young man appeared at the door. I was acutely embarrassed.

"I'm so sorry," I babbled. "We live across the hall and I had no idea you were here. Ollie!" I called out again, looking hopefully into the flat.

Nothing. Zilch response.

"Ollie, c'meer!" I ordered more determinedly, between clenched teeth.

But Ollie was on a roll. Knowing that he was in hot water, he decided he may as well be hung for a sheep as a lamb. He rampaged around, going into overdrive, and began funny running up and down the man's flat. It was like watching a Buster Keaton Movie, only with a lurcher. The man and I both watched: me in helpless horror, him in disbelief, never having seen a lurcher funny run before (it is quite a sight). Steve heard the commotion and emerged from our flat.

"What on earth?" he began.

But on seeing the look of sheer panic on my face and noting the missing lurcher, he took in the situation in a second.

"He's in there, isn't he?" Steve asked, grimly.

I could only nod and blink. Up to that point, the young man had not spoken. I continued apologizing and calling Ollie, but on finding that he had quite a good length of flat there, he continued racing up and down, around the table, underneath the table, between the chair legs, round and round.

"He'll get tired in a minute," I offered in consolation to the poor young man who, spoon in hand, was beginning to fully appreciate the unfolding situation in his flat.

Eventually, Ollie's energy was spent and he realised that he was not getting dinner. Disappointed, he flew out of the door, dodged Steve and myself as he went, nipped neatly back into our flat and hurled himself into his bed, looking mightily pleased about the whole, fabulous debacle.

"Sorry," I yelled out over my shoulder one last time as Steve and I made a shamefaced retreat and slammed our own door.

The man simply nodded, slowly closed his door and, no doubt, went back to cooking his dinner. He never uttered a word. I returned to the flat and, hands on hips, glared at Ollie who was laughing in bed.

"WHAT," I demanded, "was *that* about, you old fool?"

I had asked the lurcher the question as crossly and as insistently as I could, but it was no good. I could feel a smile forming on my face. I stole a glance at Steve: he was looking at the floor, grinning and that was it. We both collapsed laughing on the settee. Ollie was right, though: that dinner did not half smell good.

Ollie and Ralph

CHAPTER 11

Ralph

I t was so good to have Ollie home with us and despite the huge changes to his life, I knew there was very little which could faze him. I could not help but think of his sidekick, Ralph, whom I had also had the pleasure of owning. Ralph was everything Ollie was not and a perfect foil for him. I had got Ralph when he was only eight weeks old. He was a tall, elegant dog resembling an oversized greyhound. He was also clumsy and neurotic, whereas Ollie was Mister Laid Back who could not care less what was unfolding around him as long as he had a comfortable bed upon which to lie. The two were inseparable and adored each other. So how come Ralph was not with us? Let me explain.

When Ollie was about eight years old, he had become an only dog due to the unfortunate demise of my German Shepherd who, by the way, did not settle down when I got Ollie. She simply took him along with her on her travels! Anyway, urged on by my three daughters, I had decided that Ollie needed a mate. I hazily recall writing some sort of contract of agreement for the new puppy: you know the kind of thing – right, mums? That part whereby I agreed to help mum walk the pup/feed the pup/clean up after the pup – none of which happened, of course; it was all down to me.

So there in the local paper one day, I spied a litter of lurcher pups and off we went. Eight-week-old Ralph was in a box, in a somewhat dingy kitchen, with his remaining brother. He was cute beyond belief: a fawn coloured, smooth coated, snub-nosed, clumsy ball of fluff with appealing brown eyes. I should, however, have seen the writing on the wall for future neurosis as his mother *boing*-ed non-stop up and down at the kitchen window as she frantically strained to see what was occurring to her ever-decreasing family. I watched fascinated at her ability to lift off all four paws like some sort of canine *Harrier* jump jet. She never let up in her anxious attempts to be part of that deal. She would appear for a split second, wild-eyed, mouth gaping, then disappear again. I felt bad for her, I really did and wanted to tell her that I would take care of her boy and that he would be loved. And he was. Oh, he was!

To say that Ralph was accident-prone was an understatement of epic proportions. The first of many scares he gave me was at 10 weeks of age. He had gone AWOL and I was beside myself, searching high and low for that vulnerable little pup. *Where could he be?* I eventually located him. Somehow, Ralph had managed to scramble onto a kitchen chair which was padded, therefore comfortable. The chair was pushed underneath the table and he was in such a deep sleep that he had not been aware of the search and rescue drama going on around him. Lurchers, it would appear, do *not* do floors, even if they do have a fat dog bed on them. Comfort for the boys could be found squashed up together on a lounge chair – or Ralph's thinking chair as I called it. Ralph would usually clamber on first and get settled. Then there would go Ollie, first one paw, then another. Ralph would shift obligingly, making room for his big brother. There was an occasional grunt and gruff, but eventually there they would be: a happy tangle of lurchers snoozing the day away.

Ralph was a cartoon of a dog; a comic character whose personality reminded me of Scooby Doo. He may have been a couch potato indoors, but outside he was a running machine. Ollie and Ralph were a deadly dyad when it came to chasing rabbits and squirrels. I never deliberately encouraged them to chase anything, but walking the miles we did over the rolling hills of the Peak District, some casualties were unavoidable. What can I say? It was in their blood and I defy anyone to prevent a lurcher – or any dog, for that matter – from giving chase, when anything with fur on it jumped out right in front of them, then made a dash for it. I mean, it was just asking to be chased.

The speed with which Ralph tended to fly across country led to him sustaining a myriad of injuries, most of which required veterinary attention. He would race across the fields, oblivious to the jagged thorns, barbed wire and sharp stones that lay in wait to snag him. On my umpteenth visit to the vet for stitches, the latter commented that Ralph resembled a dot-to-dot picture and counted 26 scars on his smooth body. None larger than a few centimetres, mind you; but 26! Ollie rarely sustained any battle scars, being protected by his thick, wiry, tattered coat, plus he had a heap more sense.

Ralph's first, major incident occurred when he was only six months old. He was pottering in the garden and I asked one of the girls to shout him in. The task fell to my eldest daughter, Steff, who returned to report the following:

"Muuuuuum, Ralph won't come in. He's just standing there with his leg in the air."

Uh, oh! Not good. I raced out to see a sorry-looking Ralph who, for once, had the good sense not to move. On closer inspection and to my horror, I saw a deep cut, two inches long, on his front leg. I needed no veterinary training to see that it was serious – and it was Sunday. Pushing the certain knowledge of a double-sized bill to the back of my mind, I raced Ralph once again to the vet's in the nick of time. He had severed a major tendon and required immediate surgery, followed by six weeks rest and then only walks on leads. For a young, healthy pup, that was tantamount to doing time. He came out the same day with a special doggy bandage on his leg which read *Ouch, ouch, ouch* all over it – which was precisely what I said when I got the bill. OUCH!

On another occasion, I entered the lounge to see Ralph twitching and shaking his head. Puzzled, I called him. Nothing; he was out to lunch. *Sigh!* Off to the vet's again to discover he had epilepsy. It was controlled with medication, but now and again he would have a seizure, especially when stressed. When that happened, we would hold Ralph to prevent him from injuring himself, but given his size, it was akin to trying to control a six-foot-long ironing board.

Despite his propensity for accidents, injuries and seizures, Ralph was loving, generous, loyal and fun. He was also neurotic and probably autistic, if that was possible in dogs! He rarely let me out of his sight, gnawing anxiously on the closest thing to hand when worried or upset. Anything would suffice: chairs, tables, leads, arms, shoes; you name it, he would gnaw on it. He adored toys. We would buy him stuffed toys weekly from charity shops. The delight Ralph displayed in being given a new toy made us smile out loud. Steve made him a toy box in which to keep all his toys and Ralph would spend ages rooting around with his long, pointy nose until the right selection had been made. He was fiercely jealous of his toys and would growl good-naturedly if any attempt was made to steal any of them. He would then lie on the toy just in case any passing dog should happen by and spy it – well, you never knew.

Ralph loved to run and jump – boy, could he jump! I had watched repeatedly in amazement as he cleared a five-bar gate from a standstill; a talent, no doubt, inherited from his jet-propelled mother. But on occasion, he would miscalculate and end up hanging upside down by his back legs, grinning that lunatic grin of his to cries of:

"Oh, Raaalph!"

When Steve had come into my life, Ralph was six. Both Ollie and Ralph formed an immediate bond with Steve. They seemed to sense that he was a good man, one who could be trusted and loved unconditionally, and who would love them back. I had already worked that one out, but to have their seal of approval was perfect. When Steve and I first set up house, the boys were not meant to go upstairs, but that rule did not last more than five minutes. In the morning, I would peep over the banister, stifling my laughter to see Ralph creeping up the stairs with stealth and silence, hips swinging.

"Oh, no! Who's this?" I would whisper.

And despite his efforts to remain unnoticed, Ralph would give himself away, tail wagging furiously. He would barrel up the last few stairs, his cover blown, and dive onto the bed with Steve, stretching out his not inconsiderable frame – over six feet at full stretch, resembling a small kangaroo – and sigh in contentment.

"Oiii!" I would exclaim, half-heartedly. "You're not supposed to be on the bed."

Ralph would open one eye and there would be that wag again – and I would cave. Naturally, Ollie was completely aloof to such decadent behaviour. He would glare with disdain and – I swear! – he rolled his eyes more than once.

Ralph's next epic injury was to almost tear clean off one of his toes. I once again rang the vet whose number I knew by heart, only to be advised by the receptionist to pull it off!

"What??" I queried, loudly. "Pull it off? I can't do that! He's hysterical, he needs to see the vet now!"

I could almost hear the receptionist shrugging, but she begrudgingly agreed that I could take him straight in to the vet's. Pull it off, indeed! It transpired that Ralph had fractured his toe right across and once again needed surgery, that time to amputate his toe. OUCH, again!

Ralph's ever-waggy tail was the cause of him requiring even more surgery. His tail was like a whip and, unfortunately, his never-ending enthusiasm for visitors – or even if Steve or I left the room, then reappeared – was unsurpassed.

"You are HERE!"

You could almost hear Ralph say the above as he wagged up a storm. We would dodge and leap back to avoid the sting of his overzealous welcome.

"Mind his tail," we would warn visitors, usually followed by, "Sorry, sorry."

Eventually, the years of happy wagging caught up with Ralph and he damaged the end of his tail as it came into contact with cupboard doors, walls and so forth. It transpired to be a common problem with many dogs, particularly lurchers, but one that would, for us, result in a spray of cast-off blood rivalling that displayed in any good CSI crime scene. Poor Ralph! Despite the best efforts of the vet, the dog needed six inches lopped off his tail. That, however, did not deter him and his wagging and welcoming continued. It was just less painful than before for all concerned.

I now come to Ralph's last challenge: one which, tragically, not even his fortitude and resilience could overcome. My brave, loyal, beautiful lurcher developed an incurable illness. It began as a slight, but persistent, cough as if he had something stuck in his throat.

"That's not right," I would tell Steve.

Off we would go again to the vet's which, by now, had almost become our second home.

"You'll have to leave him with us for tests," the vet said that day, shaking his head in puzzlement.

A cold hand gripped my heart. The last time I had left a dog at the vet's, it had been 10 years before. My beloved first dog, Hector, was 17 years old and after being left for tests, he had never made it back home. I was paranoid about leaving dogs with vets.

"He'll be okay," reassured Steve with a hug.

"Come on, Ralph," the vet's assistant said as she took his lead.

"He won't go with you," I warned. "I'll need to bring him through for you."

"Oh, we're used to this," she smoothed.

The assistant, no doubt, thought I was some fussy owner being precious about her pet.

"He won't go," I repeated, flatly.

"Come on then, Ralphy," she repeated with some determination.

Ralphy?? I stood up. Ralph thought I was going with him, so he took a few steps. But when he took in the reality of the situation and realised, in fact, that I had stopped, he underwent one of his more famous panic states and the jump jet in him kicked in. *WHOOSH!* Up Ralph went, yanked backwards, out of his collar and ran to hide behind my legs. I raised an eyebrow at the embarrassed assistant.

"I guess you need to bring him," she conceded.

The wrench of leaving Ralph there was indescribable. Only those of you with dogs who have been your best friend can really understand how it felt. I was inconsolable. I wept and cried for Ralph with a sense of impending doom. He was 10 years old at the time and a big dog, but all those platitudes about 10 being a good age for a big dog meant nothing to me. I wanted him forever, not just for 10 years!

Ralph stayed with the vet for four agonising days. We made daily visits to him and were always greeted with furious wagging and demands to return home. Finally, the day we dreaded arrived. The vet rang us up with his findings.

"He's got megaesophagus," said the vet.

"He's got what?"

I had never heard of that. Megaesophagus, we were told, is a condition which causes dogs to regurgitate all their food and water. Other symptoms relate to the loss of calories from regurgitation or secondary pneumonia, including difficulty swallowing, excessive salivation, coughing, a change in vocal tone, nasal discharge, fever, weight loss, extreme hunger, poor body condition and respiratory distress. It can be fatal.

Ralph's case was serious. He had lost so much weight that despite being on a drip for four days, there was nothing more the vet could do. I was told that I could bring him home if I really wanted to, but that was simply delaying the inevitable. That was it, then; just like that. And you know what? It was my birthday.

I did not think I had any more fluid left in my body to produce tears, but they were endless. I clung to Steve and sobbed: great, gulping, hysterical, heart wrenching sobs. I cried aloud and punched at the wall in frustration. Steve just held me. Words were futile and unnecessary. He was trying so hard to be strong for the two of us, but he loved that dog as much as I did. In the end, we just stood there in that little kitchen and wept for Ralph together.

We eventually decided that to bring Ralph home would be a selfish decision, based solely on our needs, not his. It would also be unfair on Ollie who was sadly getting accustomed to not having Ralph around the house. Shaking every inch of the way, we made our way for the last time to the vet's. The whole experience was surreal as if I was watching from afar. I was no more than a detached spectator.

On seeing us, Ralph went into pleasure overload and that famous tail whipped to and fro. I just wanted time to stand still. It was happening too fast, I was not ready; I just was not ready for what was to ensue. I looked at Steve and saw my own agony reflected in his eyes.

"Try and get him to lie down," said the vet, quietly.

True to the last, there was no way that boy of ours was going to lie down on an uncovered hard floor. With his wits about him, Steve asked if there was a blanket that we could put down for him and a sheepskin rug appeared. Ralph lay down gratefully. He was tired and sick. He had just had enough; it was time.

A calm came over me as I stroked that beautiful head one more time and let his silky ears run through my fingers.

"You tired, mate?" I asked.

And that was it. Ralph slipped away. He left us and my grief was like a dam which suddenly burst. I do not know how long I stayed there with Ralph on the floor, holding his still warm body and willing him back to life. *Just one more walk, please; just one more walk! Oh, to see him run and jump and live again!* But, of course, that was not to be. *Ouch, ouch, ouch!*

I did not handle well the passing of our beloved lurcher, Ralph. I cried for days, weeks, months – and am crying right now as I write this down. I miss Ralph, that cartoon character of a dog, more than I could ever have known I would. But I had kept my word to his mum: he had been very much loved.

We had always known that Ralph would not make the transition to live overseas with us in Gozo. He was too neurotic for such a long car journey, too highly strung for a change of that magnitude. When he left us, we felt we had Ralph's blessing to go with his laid-back brother, Ollie, who would cope with it all – and did. But Ralph was not left behind. No way! We had him cremated and he travelled with me up front, the whole long way in his own specially made box.

Freya and Steve singing

Chapter 12

The logistics of getting to Gozo had been interesting to say the least. We had towed a two-ton trailer of belongings behind us, but that was not the half, nor the quarter, of it all. After the disaster of the lorry, we had to leave many larger items behind in storage. Those items were due to follow us, but not for several weeks.

We were now living in a more permanent flat in Marsalforn. It had taken us days to carry all our things up the three flights of stairs. It had been a Herculean task and I swear that I lost a stone in the process! Meanwhile, Ollie watched with feigned disinterest from his bed in the corner, occasionally opening an eye to make sure we were still there. Since we had brought him home from quarantine, he had been clingier than usual and reluctant to let us out of his sight. That behaviour was rather unusual for Ollie who, as a rule, was aloof and reluctant to admit that he enjoyed a cuddle and a fuss. His time away from us had changed all that. Now he kept us under constant, close surveillance – just in case.

Every corner of the flat was now crammed with sturdy flight cases which Steve had acquired from his friend in the UK. They had been absolutely brilliant. Without them, I do not really know how we would have got everything without damage. I had wrapped most of the household stuff in bubble wrap and as we unpacked, I marvelled at the weird shapes and sizes of the more delicate items.

"Guess what this is?" I would say with enthusiasm, holding up a bubbly, triangle shape.

Steve would give me a look which clearly signalled his disinterest in a game that he knew he could not win. He would then return back to the more important task of getting all his music equipment together in one place.

Over the years, Steve had amassed a huge collection of all things music. There was the big stuff: decks, amps, speakers, more amps, more speakers, rack mounts and stuff I had no idea what it was. Then there was the other stuff: unidentifiable black-box-shaped objects, all of which seemed to have an important purpose. So Steve set about organising it all to his liking – no mean feat, which took several days. Then came the leads, wires, cables, microphones, stands and goodness knows what else. Finally, there were the musical instruments: 17 guitars, all with cases; two keyboards, one set of classic drums, complete with cymbals, boxes and stands; one set of electronic drums for recording, a saxophone, a box of harmonicas, a violin, a trumpet, a clarinet, an accordion, a French horn – and a partridge in a pear tree.

With Steve's focus firmly on his music stuff, I decided to tackle the unenviable task of unpacking the clothes of which there were many; way too many. We had work on the horizon as our local guy, Mark, had booked us to sing at *The Captain's Table* within the week, so I had to locate my singing clothes. *Ah, my singing clothes!* A multi-various selection of dresses, scarves, jumpsuits, jackets, coats, boots and shoes, all of which were adorned with sparkles, sequins and shimmery bits in some form or another. My singing wardrobe was akin to the dressing-up box of a young child, but in the best possible way. It was heaven for me to own and have an excuse to wear such beautiful, often outrageous, clothes. I loved them.

Task in hand, I unpacked case after case, box after box, but did not come across any singing clothes. *Hmm,* I mused, *must be in the flight case. Yes, that was it.* I had carefully folded and packed my entire singing wardrobe and all my sparkly shoes into one giant flight case. I tracked down what I thought was the flight case and opened it up. I stared, trying to take in the scene. I shook my head and blinked as the case was unmistakeably full of leads, wires and man stuff. Not a sequin or a sparkle in sight. *No, no, that wasn't right! Where were my clothes?*

"Steve," I called out with some anxiety, "are there any big flight cases left downstairs?"

Steve was obviously lost in a world of wiry leads, amps and all things musical.

"Mmmm?" he murmured without real conviction.

I repeated the question. On hearing the words "flight case," he looked up and took notice.

"What?" Steve replied, clearly stalling for time.

"Big flight case?" I said for the third time. "The one with all my clothes in it. Where is it?"

Steve pursed his lips in thought and I thought I saw a shadow of worry pass across his face.

"What's the matter?" I asked. "I can't find my singing clothes, but I know they're all in that last, big flight case."

There was a discernible flinch.

"You flinched!" I accused.

"No, I didn't," Steve denied.

"Yes, yes, you did!" I replied. "What's the matter? Where are my clothes and shoes?"

Steve studied the ground for a few moments, then inspected his fingernails. Then he seemed to gain sudden pleasure from the view out of the window and took to staring over the valley.

Silence.

"Steve," I said, slowly and deliberately. "Where. Are. My. Clothes?"

Steve sighed. It was evident that he knew something I did not.

"Ermmm, I think, that was one of the flight cases we had to leave in storage," he finally replied.

There was a pregnant pause as my mind struggled to take in that gem of information. I opened my mouth and shut it again, knowing that I probably looked like a goldfish. No sound came out. I tried again.

"We??" I managed.

"Err, yes. Well, you know we couldn't get everything in. I had to leave a big flight case behind," Steve finally admitted in muted tones.

"You did what? You left my clothes behind?" I reiterated unnecessarily as the enormity of the situation dawned on me in all its glorious horror. "You left my CLOTHES?" I squawked with great indignation. "What am I supposed to wear for the gigs??!"

Steve shuffled his feet and looked subdued.

"You've got loads of stuff to sing in," he offered.

"Not here I don't! Everything's in that flight case," I reiterated with vehemence.

"Ah," Steve said. "Ah!" as the realisation finally visited him. "Aah," he repeated in the apparent absence of any other available words.

"Well, I can bet you diamonds, you didn't leave any guitars, amps, speakers or wires behind," I fumed. "No, I'm absolutely certain all YOUR stuff is here!" I continued, the bit between my teeth now. "Oh, no! Leave MY stuff AND you made me leave the microwave!" I accused, on a roll and with clear grudges to air. "And my food mixer," I continued, "but looka here, whaddya know, all your stuff. Right here, all present and correct, hmm?!"

"Ah!" said Steve. "Mmm, sorry."

But he did not look sorry one bit. In fact, Steve looked suspiciously relieved that he had all his stuff. Men!

So that was it. I had to go and find a shop which sold sparkly dresses and shoes, and spend some of what remained of our dwindling savings. It was not too great a hardship really and I discovered, to my delight, that Gozo had a great selection of independent boutiques which sold some amazing, inexpensive clothes. It transpired that on the island there were many festivals all year round and the local people loved dressing up and celebrating in style. They were well catered for, therefore, with the shops demonstrating a strong Italian influence, given the island's close proximity to Italy. Steve's guilt was in full swing and I was soon decked out with a couple of new dresses and a pair of shoes, until the container arrived with the abandoned flight case and the rest of our belongings.

We finally got the call we had been waiting for in February 2011. Our container had reached Malta and would be with us within five days. Now arose the problem of where to put a container-load of enormous flight cases, one jukebox and a 600cc motorbike. We need not have worried, though. We had forged more friendships in Gozo than we had ever made in the UK and through those friendships, we were given access to a disused building that would easily accommodate all the things we needed to store.

We were extremely relieved when the *Gozo Express* lorry trundled into Marsalforn, reuniting us with our shipment. The men could not have been more helpful in offloading the heavy, numerous flight cases and motorbike. Eventually, all was completed and the cases were safe in the building, ready for the epic task of unpacking them. Our enthusiasm in rediscovering our stuff was sadly short-lived as we realised with dismay that we were missing many things.

Unsurprisingly, Steve had a comprehensive collection of *Dr Who* and *Star Trek* figures and collectables, which he had amassed over the four years we had been together. All were in mint condition and boxed, but well over 80% of them were now missing. In addition, many of Steve's lifetime-of-Elvis memorabilia collection were also gone: pictures, figures and a host of other items; all gone. As the stuff had been in storage in the UK, then moved by lorry to the dock and sailed to Malta in a cargo vessel before making its final journey in yet another lorry, we had no idea at what point in the journey the things had been 'liberated.' It was a bitter disappointment, but a lesson learned. Although sturdy, the flight cases had not been locked and were, therefore, easily accessible to anyone who fancied a rummage through them. We knew that in future, we would have to padlock and wrap any and all cases, to avoid such a thing from happening again.

All of the above aside, we were delighted to be able to take things back to the flat, to make it more homely – not least, I had my clothes and shoes again. Thankfully, I could only assume that they were not to the taste of the people who had helped themselves to our other items. Or, maybe, they just did not fit.

CHAPTER 13

Gozo

We have been repeatedly asked how we just "went to Gozo." Was it easy? Did we need a visa? What was the weather like in winter? What was there to do? And so on. So I think it is time to reflect a bit on, and try to answer, some of the questions we have been asked. What follows is a reflection of *our* experiences and thoughts. Other people will, undoubtedly, have different ideas of what life is like in Gozo, which will be unique to themselves.

Malta joined the European Union (EU) in May 2004. Consequently, Gozo is also part of the EU since it is one of the Maltese Islands. Citizens of full European member countries (EEA, EFTA) can live and work in Malta and Gozo without the need for a visa or work permit. Size wise, Malta is 16.8 miles long by nine miles wide. In comparison, Gozo is a mere nine miles long by four and a half miles wide, so it is considerably smaller than its big sister, Malta. Figures produced at the end of 2012 showed that Malta had a population of just over 421,000, while approximately 31,000 people call Gozo home. Given the ratio of square miles to people, Malta has a high population density. We would not have chosen to live in Malta as although it is beautiful, it was too crowded and busy for us.

Malta and Gozo are predominantly Roman Catholic (98%) in religion, boasting some of the most beautiful churches you could ever find anywhere in the world, both in architecture and décor. Malta has 313 churches, Gozo has 46. The church in Xewkija, Gozo can comfortably accommodate a population of 3000 and has a dome larger than that of Saint Paul's in London.

Finding a place to live in Gozo is fairly straightforward. There are several estate agents on the island who can arrange long-term rentals (six months or more), but we found that many Gozitans own more than one property, which they are only too happy to rent out long-term. During our time of living in Gozo, Steve and I lived in a total of four properties: two apartments and two farmhouses. One was arranged for us through an estate agent and three were rented directly from the owners. Prices ranged from around 200 euros a month for a decent three bedroom, two bathroom apartment, right up into the thousands for a large, detached villa with pool. It paid to shop around and negotiate the price as owners were often willing to take less rent if the tenant was going to be there for over six months. If you rent via an estate agent, you will pay a fee.

The climate in Gozo was a main attraction to Steve and myself. The average yearly temperature of Malta is around 23° Celsius during the day and 16° Celsius at night, one of the highest in Europe. In the coldest month, January, the typically maximum temperature ranged from 12° Celsius to 20° Celsius during the day and a minimum range of 7° Celsius to 12° Celsius at night. In the warmest month, August, the typically maximum temperature ranged from 28° Celsius to 34° Celsius during the day and a minimum range of 20° Celsius to 24° Celsius at night.

We moved to Gozo in December. The weather was obviously warmer than in the UK where we had left snowstorms, ice and freezing temperatures behind us. We were hugely relieved to find some sunshine in Gozo and spent every spare minute outside on the roof of the flat, soaking it up. January saw more clouds moving in and while we still managed a few hours of sunbathing almost daily, we started feeling chilly especially when we went inside. Many of the flats and apartments in Gozo are large and open plan. That was great in summer, but in winter we soon discovered that they were not only Baltic but costly to heat.

By February, we were huddled together underneath a blanket on the settee, watching the rain fall incessantly. We later discovered that the rain in February 2011 was close to a record for Malta: something like the second highest rainfall ever. Well, it would be; wouldn't it?! We were beginning to ask ourselves:

"What on earth have we done?"

We were cold all the time and fighting a never-ending battle against damp and mould. As most flats in Malta and Gozo do not have central heating or fireplaces, although some do, a lot of people rely on calor gas heaters to warm up the place. A small bottle of calor gas cost approximately 16 euros and, on average, lasted about a week. It was not an economical way to heat the flat and only added to the damp as it caused high levels of condensation. The fumes also made our eyes and throats sore.

What was convenient, though, was that a calor gas deliveryman drove around as regular as clockwork every Wednesday morning, blasted his horn and left you more gas. What was even more remarkable was that we regularly left our empty gas bottle outside, with an envelope containing our 16 euros tucked into it and no one would dream of stealing it. Forgive my cynicism, but I cannot envisage a similar scenario in the UK. But the damp was horrendous and led to us having to throw away a lot of clothes, bedding and pillows as they turned a lovely shade of green which did not wash out despite my best efforts. When dressing in the morning, our clothes felt so damp and cold, it was horrible, so we took to using the hairdryer to warm them up – *not* what we had in mind when we originally moved to Gozo. We quickly learned that a dehumidifier was an essential piece of equipment as the biggest fear of ours was that Steve's valuable music equipment would be ruined. We duly purchased one and emptied it without fail twice a day as the condensation and humidity were so high. The damp also affected Steve's health and he ended up spending several days in *Gozo Hospital* with bad chest infections. He eventually acclimatised, but that took many months.

We had not been prepared for those conditions, naively thinking that it would be warm all year round and it did cause us to question whether that was the place in which to be. However, we also realised that there were many ways to manage the environment in which we lived and once we had got to grips with putting up curtains to keep the heat in, ditching the calor gas, using electric heaters and opening the windows as often as possible to allow the air to circulate, things became more comfortable. Add to that the fact that the majority of the time in Gozo it *was* warm or, better still, hot, we decided that we had not just made the biggest mistake of our lives and would continue living there.

Food shopping in Gozo offered lots of choice. There were small shops in pretty much all the villages. There were also visiting grocers vans and bread vans – part of daily life – with horns blaring to announce their arrival early in the morning. Victoria is the capital of Gozo and home to many well-known shops. Among others there is a *Next, Dorothy Perkins, Mothercare, New Look, George* and, of course, *McDonalds*. I swear, those last will be the first fast food outlet on Mars! There were also many good independent shops, boutiques and beauty salons, and plenty of cafés, bars and restaurants. There were several larger supermarkets in Victoria, which easily compared to the small versions of main UK supermarkets. In April 2014, a new *Lidl* opened in Gozo and was proving to be extremely popular. Most places were well stocked and offered pretty much everything we needed. However, buying UK brands could be rather expensive.

Our weekly shopping bill was, overall, more expensive than in the UK, but while many UK brands were at a premium, many items were cheaper. Meat was particularly reasonable, although we ate mainly chicken. I will never forget the first time I asked for two chicken breasts at the supermarket. The assistant picked up an entire double chicken breast from the pile in front of her.

"Two?" she asked, piling another one on.

In reality, that equated to four of what I had asked for and they were enormous, but I did not wish to say 'no.'

"Perfect," I smiled, thinking it was a good job we had a freezer.

The whole lot was just a reasonable 4.50 euros.

Fruit and veg were often straight from someone's allotment and tasted as they should. Carrots, potatoes, tomatoes often came complete with dirt and needed washing before you could use them. When you have been in the habit of shopping at a UK supermarket, where every single thing has been scrubbed and wrapped in plastic, it came as a bit of a shock to be presented with grubby leeks which had long, tatty ends on them; dirt-encrusted carrots and, maybe, a slug or two in your lettuce and green veg.

The first time we ate carrots in Gozo, I actually told Steve, "Hey, they actually taste of carrots."

It sounds absurd, I know, but in the UK you would be paying premium prices for *Best Ever* or *Taste the Difference,* if you wanted veg to taste as it should. One word of caution, though. We did find – or rather, I found as Steve did not venture into the kitchen – that goods such as flour, rice, lentils and so on could end up being infested with critters! I use *Basmati* rice and, thankfully, always soak it before cooking. The first time I did that in Gozo, I thought I was seeing things as there were, floating about, hundreds of what looked like husks. On closer inspection, I was horrified to find that they were bugs, specifically weevils. It happened again two years later when I was about to eat some cereal. Thankfully, I had looked down at the bowl before starting to eat and noticed something moving. Somehow, moths had got into the box. I never ate cereal in Gozo again! Weevils and bugs seemed to be able to get into everything and despite our using sealed plastic containers for everything, they still managed to find a way in. My guess was that they got in at source as, in the case of the cereal, it was a brand new pack.

Eating out in Gozo was most definitely cheaper than in the UK. Even in the more touristy areas of the island, where prices were inevitably higher, it was still cheaper than in the UK. Steve and I could easily go for a delicious, freshly made pizza; an *Angus* burger with fries and onion rings, a large glass of very decent wine and a *Coke* for around 10 euros. A more elaborate meal of, say, a starter, followed by chicken or steak dinner with sides along with drinks, would cost no more than 35 euros for both of us. A lesser snack of two ham-and-cheese toasties and two coffees could be had for as little as three euros in total if you knew where to go. Most villages in Gozo have what is known as a band club. These were inevitably the cheapest places at which to eat and have a drink, and while some of them may not have been terribly auspicious in décor, they were friendly, cheap and well worth a visit. And yes, bands do practice in Gozo – the brass variety!

Shopping for clothes was variable, depending on where you went. On the whole, I was impressed with the price and quality of the clothes and shoes available for sale in Gozo. Conversely, white goods and kitchen equipment were extremely expensive. How I came to regret leaving my microwave in the UK! The cheapest one we managed to find in Gozo was 65 euros, compared and comparable to a *Tesco* basic £25 model.

We found it tricky to take things back to shops when needed as even with a receipt, we were, at times, met with a shrug and, "What can you do?"

In our experience, most shops would not give refunds, but offered to fix things or give credit notes. One particular incident springs to mind. I wanted a simple food processor to make pastry. I did not want to spend a lot and said that to the shop assistant.

"I only need to make about half a pound of pastry at a time," I explained.

Shown to me was a seemingly reasonably-priced processor at 34 euros. *Yes, a bit cheap and plasticky, but it will do,* I thought. I tried not to think about my *Kenwood Chef* processor which I had somewhat begrudgingly donated to a charity shop in Mabelthorpe. More so, I pushed from my mind the new owner who, in the first place, could not believe their luck at such a find in a charity shop and who was, undoubtedly, making pound after pound of incomparable pastry in it.

Anyway, I was assured that this lesser model would do the job, so I took it home, eager to make Steve his beloved cheese-and-onion pie. I measured out the ingredients, half a pound in total, switched it on and away it went. *Bzzzzzz.* It managed about 10 seconds, then gave up. I pressed the processor, shook it, scraped the mixture down and tried again and again, but it was no use. The food processor was simply not man or woman enough for the task. *Sigh!* I cleaned it up and went back to the shop, receipt in hand.

"This mixer is no good," I began. "I was told it would easily mix pastry, but it won't. It's conked out."

I was regarded as though I had just entered the shop and threatened to single-handedly declare war on the whole of Gozo.

"Yes?" came the completely disinterested reply.

"Well, I'd like a refund ideally," I continued, "but I don't mind buying a better model and putting more money to it, but this won't do."

The woman sniffed and looked at the mixer.

"It is used?" she declared, accusingly. "You've used it. I cannot exchange used goods."

I stared and frowned, but remembering about the wrinkle thing again, I stopped.

"Of course, it's used! That's how I know it's no good!" I exclaimed.

"I cannot exchange used goods," repeated the woman, haughtily.

"So what are my options then," I queried.

"We fix it for you," she explained.

"But that won't change how powerful it is," I replied, stating the obvious. "It's simply not powerful enough and I really would like another one."

"Madam, it's been used and I can't issue a refund on it. We'll fix it and ring you."

I never got to see that food processor again.

Fuel costs in Gozo are about the same as in the UK, so no big difference there. I have briefly touched on bringing a car over to Malta, but just to reiterate, you would need to do some homework if you plan on taking a car or motorbike as there are charges which can be prohibitive. It all depends on the size of the engine and the age of the vehicle. It also makes a difference if it is a commercial vehicle.

We had a 10-year-old, six cylinder, 2.6 litres *Vauxhall Vectra*, which if we had registered it, would have set us back a whopping 1200 euros, with an additional 900 euros annually for road tax, which would have increased each year as the vehicle aged. Small wonder that we did not bother and, after a 12-month exemption, we sadly ended up scrapping a perfectly good car for 100 euros as we could not justify the massive cost of registering it in the Maltese Islands.

An additional bonus to being in Gozo was that most people spoke English. I confess that I tried learning some Gozitan (the Maltese and Gozitan languages differ slightly), but I found it an extremely complicated and difficult language to learn. I was able to manage a few phrases here and there, but on the whole I was grateful that English was spoken in most places. I was also grateful that people drove on the left like in the UK, so I did not have to worry about remembering to get *that* right every time I went out.

Another huge factor for us was the wonderful welcome we were given not only by the expat community, but by local Gozitans. We encountered a warmth and friendliness that endeared us to the people and to that magical island, and which became a major contributing factor in our wanting to make Gozo our permanent home.

In our first few months on the little island, we learned a lot. We knew the best places to shop and where to eat out. We knew better than to rely on calor gas as a means of heating the flat and realised that a dehumidifier was essential. We sadly came to accept that taking things back to shops was really *not* worth the hassle. On the plus side, we knew our way around, where to sit and where to enjoy the most breathtaking sunsets. We discovered beautiful walks, with the hair-raising scramble down from

Għajnsielem to the tiny bay of Mġarr ix-Xini being our favourite. In 2015, Brad Pitt and Angelina Jolie took over that tiny bay for the making of their latest movie. It was out of bounds for several months, but I now hear that it is back to normal, with an understandable increase in interest and tourists.

We marveled at the history of Gozo and sampled the local cuisine and fabulous wines. Best of all, we made many friends, both local Gozitans and expats. In a nutshell, we felt at home. We had no regrets and zero desire to return back to the UK. So far, therefore, the grass was most definitely greener although it still needed some mowing.

Steve with Ollie in the quarantine pen

CHAPTER 14

I awoke to the familiar sound of heavy rain. It had gone on for weeks. I opened one eye and in a test of temperature, exposed one hand from underneath the covers to the elements of the flat. *Brr! That did not feel warm at all.* Still, we were not yet at the end of February, so we could expect more rain and gloomy conditions.

I needed coffee, but did not want to leave the cosy sanctuary of the bed where Steve still lay blissfully unaware of the dismal day which dawned. As I contemplated making coffee, I wondered if it would dry up enough later in the day to peg out my washing – a humdrum thing to be considering, but one which had to be addressed. Having access to the roof meant that I could usually peg out all the washing up there. Steve had also kitted me out with a new washing line for that very purpose. It had proved interesting, implementing that process in high winds, and more than one of Steve's shirts had never been seen again after I forgot to bring it in when the winds picked up. Other items had not infrequently been found neatly folded on our front step, returned to us by kind farmers who ran across them in their fields across the way and who knew that they belonged to that stupid Englishwoman who did not know any better than to hang out her washing in gale force winds.

Reluctantly, I emerged from my nest and made coffee, staring out over the valley as I sipped it and felt the caffeine course through my veins. How I loved my Italian filter coffee! It was most definitely my drug of choice. Although the rain was lashing down, I could not help discerning some beauty in the misty curtain it formed. I knew that when it ceased, the valley would be greener for it and look lush and healthy, rather than brown and dry as in the summer months.

Ah, well. Better get ready and take Ollie out, I thought. I knew he would not appreciate the outing. Ollie, like his sadly missed brother, Ralph, was a fair-weather lurcher. He did not go out in the rain unless absolutely essential and had demonstrated his incredible powers of bodily control on the 1700-mile trip to Gozo – apart, that is, when he was on the Genova ferry. No, Ollie would rather lie in his bed and beetle to the door in his own good time, when a toilet break was required.

"C'mon, mister," I encouraged. "Let's have you. Time to go out."

Ollie surveyed me furtively. There was no movement.

"I know you're awake, matey. Come on, you've got to go out," I continued.

Ollie concentrated on ignoring me altogether and curled up tighter in his bed. He might have been 19, but there was absolutely nothing wrong with his hearing – and he could hear that rain.

"No, thank you," he seemed to say. "I'm staying here."

I persisted.

"Ollie, it's no use ignoring me. We're going out, like it or not. Now come ON."

Ollie shifted his weight slightly, opened both eyes and gave me a shrewd look. We stared at each other for a minute or so, until he sighed and did one of those marvellous screamy yawns that dogs do – you know, when they yawn and a sort of a yowl comes out at the same time. That was a screamy yawn in our house! He stood up and stretched and, oh, ever so reluctantly followed me to the door.

We made our way carefully down the stairs of which there were more than 50, which was no mean feat for an old guy like Ollie. It was, actually, also no mean feat for Steve and myself as we knew, to our cost, whenever we brought shopping back with us to the flat.

"Why did we have to buy all this?" Steve would complain as he laboured up the stairs, knowing there were two more trips until we had it all upstairs.

Water was the worst culprit as despite the bad weather, you still had to drink a lot of water since the humidity was high. It was fairly cheap at around two euros for a total of six two-litre bottles, but when you bought three packs at a time . . . . . Well, you get the picture.

Ollie and I stepped out and were immediately struck by the force of the wind and the rain. The lurcher was nothing if not efficient: he did what he needed to do in double quick time and we both scooted back gratefully up the stairs to the warmth of the flat. As the day progressed, the weather brightened up, the sun made an appearance and I decided to put out the washing. Off to the roof I went – and did a double take. *What was that?* My washing line had disappeared; it simply was not there. I looked around the roof in the futile hope that it had fallen down, but I knew that Steve had tied it up securely. Good grief, the man's DIY prowess was legendary and to suggest there was any fault in his washing line hanging would be inconceivable. Even thinking it – let alone saying it out loud – would provoke indignation of the highest order. So I peered over the edge, stifling an attack of vertigo. Nope. No sign. *What on earth?* I returned back down and into the flat.

"Steve," I began, "I know this is a stupid question, but you haven't seen my washing line, have you? It's not there."

Steve looked up from the important and seemingly never-ending task of wire sorting.

"What?" he asked, incredulously. "What do you mean, your washing line's not there? Where is it?" shaking his head in disbelief.

"I've no idea," I continued. "It's gone. Vanished, disappeared," I added in a blatant overuse of adjectives.

Steve stood up and moved to the door, his intent clear. *He* would check the roof for the stray washing line as, clearly, my observational skills were lacking. Up we went, together. Steve did a cursory sweep of the roof and I was demoted to being a bystander. Then Steve put his army training to good use and undertook a more thorough search using a clear grid pattern, left to right, right to left, before turning to me.

He declared, "It's not here."

I sucked in my teeth, trying not to laugh.

"I know," I agreed with a solemn nod.

We both stood on the roof in the wasted sunshine, confounded as to where the washing line had gone. At the end, we gave up and went back down into the flat. As I closed the door, I happened to look across at the neighbour's flat.

"She's got her washing hanging outside her door," I noticed aloud. "That's a good idea if it's raining," I added without thinking as I saw the washing festooned on the railings.

Hang on a minute! I looked again and again . . . . . I could not believe my eyes. There, hanging outside, tied up good and tight with *her* washing on it, was my washing line! I stared in amazement. *Yes, it was mine!* Bright blue and brand new, and clearly not on the roof where it should have been. I shut the door quickly.

"Steve," I hissed, "guess what?"

Steve had returned to the wire-sorting task and showed mild irritation at being disturbed once again.

"What is it?" he mumbled.

"It's my washing line," I said in a conspiratorial whisper. "The woman next door has it hanging outside her flat with *her* washing on it. Look!" pointing and opening the door a crack to reassure myself that I was not seeing things.

"You're kidding me!" said Steve in disbelief.

"No, no! Really, look!" I exclaimed in hushed tones as I opened the door with a flourish so that Steve could see clearly for himself. "That's it, right there!" triumphantly.

"Well, of all the cheek!" exclaimed Steve, offended at such a clear breach of laundry etiquette.

By that time, I was laughing at the ridiculousness of it all.

"What shall we do?" I giggled.

"Do? Do??" spluttered Steve. "I'll tell you what I'll do! I'll go across there right now and I'll . . . . ."

I think, dear reader, that Steve's intended actions are best not put into print at this point. Suffice it to say that I soothed him and managed to distract Steve by reminding him that he had a lot of wires requiring his immediate attention. I also promised that I would go over to the neighbour and sort out what I was sure was a misunderstanding – although quite how you misunderstand what is and what is not your washing line, I was not quite sure.

"Hmmm. Well, okay," said Steve, torn by his protective duties to me and his wire sorting. "But if you have any trouble, any trouble at all, you come get me, you hear?" he said as he applied himself once again to wire world.

I knocked on the door of the neighbour, staring at my washing line as I did so.

"Soon have you back on the roof," I told it, somewhat unnecessarily.

I immediately felt foolish, talking to a length of nylon. Meanwhile, a woman appeared at the door. She looked at me blankly and said nothing.

"Hi, there," I began, "I think there's been some mistake here. You seem to have my washing line," pointing at the line and smiling in what I was confident was a neighbourly smile.

The woman shook her head and said something in Gozitan. *Oh, great. Just great!* She spoke as much English as I did Gozitan.

I pointed again at the washing line, tapped my chest and simply said, "Mine," a bit possessively.

I think the chest tapping was probably a bit over the top, but it was, after all, the truth. Thankfully, another lady appeared who did speak English. I explained again that it was my washing line. There followed an exchange between the two women in Gozitan, whereafter the English-speaking lady turned to me.

"It was raining, so she had to hang her washing inside," the lady said.

I blinked.

"Err, okay," I replied with some hesitation. "But she took my washing line down from the roof to do so and I'd like it back."

More dialogue ensued and I fancied that it started sounding a bit angry. The woman turned to me somewhat impatiently.

"Yes, yes. She has only borrowed it as it was raining."

It seemed that this was all the explanation I was going to get. Time for more direct tactics.

"Well, I'd like it back now, please," I stated, folding my arms in defiance.

No one moved or spoke.

"Now, please!" I repeated, looking at the offending washing line.

Both women rolled their eyes as if my request was the singularly, most unrealistic utterance they had ever heard. They half-heartedly removed the washing then disappeared inside, shaking their heads and scolding me in Gozitan for the inconvenience I had apparently caused them in demanding back my own washing line.

Naturally, I could not get the damned thing untied from the railings and had to shout for Steve who was just waiting to be called on to intervene. He had the situation assessed in a millisecond and reappeared, Swiss army knife in hand. With one deft sweep, he liberated the line from its wrongful home.

"There," he said with great satisfaction. "Hmm. Sharp knife, that," he mused as we went back in and, thankfully, shut the door.

"It's brightened up quite a lot," I said later that day, washing firmly on the line on the roof. "Shall we take Ollie for a good walk?"

Despite his lethargy in bad weather, Ollie did enjoy his walks when it was fine and showed great enthusiasm when the occasion called for it. So it was agreed that we would take him alongside the dry riverbed in Marsalforn, where we could safely let him off his lead for a run – yes, he could still run, even at his advanced age. When we got down there, however, we were astonished at the sight we met. The weeks of heavy rain had turned what had been a dry riverbed into a raging torrent. It was a spectacular sight to see. What had been stones, dust and weeds now resembled whitewater rapids. In my lifetime, I have had several dogs who would have leapt into that water with glee and gusto, but Ollie was not among them. At the risk of repeating myself, lurchers do not, as a rule, do water. They do not do damp and they do not do slightly moist. In short, they are wusses who like the warm comfort of a bed – preferably yours – and do not, under any circumstances, lie on a floor unless there are absolutely no other options available. It was, therefore, with some confidence that I let Ollie off his lead, knowing that he would avoid the water at any cost.

Given the weeks of rain, it had been some time since Ollie had been on a really good, long walk where he could get off his lead and have a good run. Off he went, sniffing and snuffling around at the new smells of that unfamiliar, soggy world. All of a sudden, he decided to go for it and set off at a run. We watched, laughing as he raced happily around. However, he then decided to put into high gear and try one of his famous funny runs.

Ollie was about 200 yards away and heading straight for us at a flat out run, tail tucked under and that stupid grin on his face. As he approached, we took in the unfolding situation and realised with horror that he was going way too fast to make the bend which was approaching.

"Slow down, mate! Slow down!" I yelled.

But it was no use. Ollie was committed and I could hardly bear to watch.

"He's not going to make it!" I shrieked at Steve who stood speechless as he waited for the inevitable.

Too late, Ollie realised his error. He was most definitely not going to make the bend and with no emergency braking system, he started to back pedal, frantically scrabbling with his gazelle-like legs to abort the run. No use. The lurcher careered off track like some demented cartoon character and skidded sideways *straight* into the raging river.

Kersplosh!! Pandemonium broke out. Ollie gasped and began struggling in the freezing water which was, at least, five feet deep. In his 19 years, I had never seen him even paddle in water and while I know that all animals have an inbuilt ability to swim, it was not his forte and he was an old dog with limited energy and reserves. I knew we had to get him out fast.

"DO SOMETHING!" I shouted to Steve who stood staring, aghast. "Steve, save him!"

No use. Steve was not moving fast enough for my liking, so I raced forward to attempt my own rescue.

"Be careful," warned Steve.

But I was deaf to it all. The only thing I could think of was getting Ollie out. I got to the edge and the poor old boy resembled the proverbial drowned rat. His front legs flailed around as he tried to swim for the first time in his life.

"Ollie, over here," I called.

But he was lost, circling and splashing around in panic. I started climbing down to grab him, but after all that rain, it was awfully slippery and . . . . *Kersplosh!!* I joined him in the water. *Oh. My. God. How cold was it in there?*

"Steve, Steve!" I cried, gasping with the shock of the cold water as I grabbed for Ollie and, thankfully, managed to get hold of his collar. "Help us!"

Steve was galvanised into action. There was nothing for it; the situation had escalated beyond control. He had to slide down into the Arctic waters and take a half-drowned lurcher from my grasp, depositing him on the banks before dragging me out. Ollie shook himself off, ragingly indignant at the unasked-for bath. He then set off at a furious pace, funny running up and down in a futile attempt to get dry. Steve was shaking his head in despair.

"What on earth were you thinking?" he chastised. "I knew you were going to fall in," he continued, piously. "You're so impatient! I was just assessing the safest way to get Ollie out, but you had to panic and go rushing in there."

I was speechless, but only for a second.

"What??" I said in disbelief. "You just stood there, doing nothing," I reiterated, affronted. "Someone had to help him," I added with a touch of the burning martyr in my voice.

Steve's eyes widened.

"I told you, I was about to take action. But oh, no! Here you come, blundering in and complicating the situation," he responded.

There then followed a sharp debate as Steve and I held a post mortem on what just happened and who should have done what. All the while, Ollie was performing superb funny runs, oblivious to our upset. Eventually, Steve sat down, took off his extremely expensive cowboy boots and emptied the water out of them.

"Look at my good boots!" he scowled. "Ruined!"

In my peripheral vision, I saw Ollie perform another fly by. Suddenly, I saw the funny side of it. No one was hurt. Ollie was wet and cold, and extremely peed off, but he was okay. I started laughing.

"What the ****?" said Steve as he sat there wetly on a rock in his stockinged feet.

"Did you see his face when he realised he wasn't going to make it?" I replied, doubling over at the memory of it.

"Stupid dog," said Steve, darkly.

But I could see that he was cracking.

"Ollie, for goodness sake, calm down now," he said as Ollie made one more pass.

We eventually caught the lurcher and all three of us walked coldly and wetly home. Once in the flat, Steve and Ollie went first into the shower. Ollie's fury was unsurpassed. To get wet by accident was one thing, but to have to be subject to a deliberate soaking was the limit. He sulked for days. We could finally laugh about it.

Showered and dry, we continued smiling at the memory of our unforgettable day. We decided to go out to eat and relived Ollie's dunking one more time over dinner.

"What a day!" I said, emphatically.

"I know," agreed Steve.

"What else can go wrong, eh?"

Steve laughed. We stayed out late and got back to the flat at around 1.00am. It was dark, but reliably, Steve had a torch. He dropped me at the front door, while he went to park the car across the road. I knew the key was a bit dodgy in the main entrance lock, but it was being particularly awkward that night – or rather, that very early morning. I wiggled and jiggled it in the lock, but the door would not open. I could see Steve approaching and did not want him to arrive, to find that I had not even got the door open yet.

"What's up?" Steve asked as he strolled up.

"Stupid key won't open the door again," I muttered and gave it one last, good turn. "Oh, come ON," I snarled, giving it a particularly savage twist.

There was an ominous snapping sound as the key buckled under that unasked-for abuse and I found myself standing with just the top of it in my hand. I bit my lip and closed my eyes. As it was dark, Steve could not see what had just happened.

"Let me try," he offered.

I drew in a deep breath before launching into my defence speech.

"Ha, ha! You know how you said at dinner what else could go wrong? Ha, ha! Well, you're not going to believe this," I stuttered. "It's a funny thing, but this key, well, I think the metal must have got, well, metal fatigue or something, with all the jiggling in the lock and, well . . . . ."

"You've broken it, haven't you?" Steve interrupted, flatly.

"Yes," I said in a small voice. "Sorry."

"Right," came the strangled response. "Of course, all my tools are inside and I can't get to them."

We stood there in the dark, with the torchlight illuminating the lock and highlighting my heavy-handed mistake.

"I could ring the owner," I suggested, throwing us a lifeline.

The owner of the flat thankfully ran a nearby bar and kept late hours. I am extremely grateful to report that he was just about to close up and willingly came down to help. With the right tools for the job, Steve had the trapped key out in no time and the owner let us in with his master key. We had never been so glad to get into bed and put that day and night behind us. I was just drifting into blissful sleep when Steve prodded me.

"Mmm, what is it?" I said, sleepily.

"I think Ollie needs to go out," replied Steve.

And I could tell by the tone of his voice that he was smiling out loud. As for Ollie, his revenge was complete.

CHAPTER 15

Hurling three cushions off the sofa and across the room, Steve asked, "What are we doing today?"

I winced. Like many women, I love lots of fat, fluffy cushions. I particularly like fat, fluffy cushions with sequins and sparkly bits on them, and like many men, Steve does not like them. His dislike extends to pillow cases with sparkles on, which he pointedly turns over so that he is lying on the unadulterated side. That manoeuvre is usually accompanied by a pained look and a sigh. In relation to the cushions, he would sit down on the sofa, scowl in vexation, reach behind him, look at me accusingly as if I had left a deadly scorpion for him to sit on, then fling the offending articles across the room. He would inevitably add:

"Do we HAVE to have all these things? I can hardly fit on here for cushions."

I would be highly affronted, retrieve the rejected missiles and sulk. The cushions were eventually banished to the car boot sale where I could be heard muttering about the price I had paid for them at Dunelm, in comparison to the two euros each that they realised in Gozo. Apparently, Gozitan men are not cushions fans, either.

We had by now moved out of our temporary flat in Marsalforn, into a larger, more spacious, second floor apartment in Għajnsielem (vaguely pronounced Ain-Seal-Em). We had yet to drag all our belongings up the two flights of stairs and knew that we were only delaying the inevitable. Most of our things were stored in a lock-up in Marsalforn and as it was a nice day, we agreed to go and bring more items back to the flat.

When we got there, Steve immediately became distracted with trying to start his 600cc *Suzuki Bandit* motorbike. The bike had been delivered along with a container-load of other goods and had, to date, registered its protest at being moved to such a damp climate by refusing to start. Steve manhandled the bike outside and began tinkering with it as I sat in the early March sunshine, enjoying the stunning views over the sea.

On hearing a car approach, I turned to see one of the familiar white *Mercedes* taxis which serve the island, coming down the hill. The driver caught sight of Steve and his bike, and without hesitation, pulled over and parked. He got quickly out of the car, his eyes shining like those of a fanatic.

"This is your bike, yes?" he asked, enthusiastically.

Steve looked up, startled. He had not heard the man approaching.

"Yes, it's mine," replied Steve replied, proffering his hand in greeting.

The taxi driver slowly circled the bike with great reverence.

"This is, indeed, a wonderful machine," he said with approval. "My brother, he had a similar one, but not as big as this one. Will you sell it to me?" he added, hopefully.

Steve looked taken aback. He had not expected that and searched tactfully for the right words.

"Err, well, it's not actually running very well at the moment and I hadn't considered selling it. Not yet, anyway," he explained.

The man mournfully shook his head.

"If you wish to sell it, you must ring me and I . . . . . I will come! I will get in my car and drive to you," he declared, theatrically. "Here, I give you my number."

The man reached into his pocket for a business card. At that point, the car window opened and a head popped out.

"Can we please go now?" asked an irritated female voice.

Steve and I looked on in amazement. The driver actually had a fare in the back of the taxi, yet had stopped to chat to Steve about the bike. The driver assumed a pained expression and turned to the woman.

"In a minute," he said in troubled tones. "I am conducting business here, if you don't mind."

The taxi driver resumed his discussion with Steve, repeating his promise to come immediately if Steve were to change his mind. The plaintive voice of the woman floated over again from the back seat.

"I have to get to Victoria," she pressed.

The driver rolled his eyes as if that were a great inconvenience and unwillingly returned to his vehicle.

"Call me!" he shouted as he drove away. "I will come!"

Steve and I exchanged amused glances and returned back to what we had been doing.

The episode put us in mind of a similar incident which had happened the week before. Steve and I had become friends with another taxi driver whom, for the purpose of this book, I shall call Joseph. Well, when I say "we" had become friends, it was more that Joseph adopted Steve, while I may as well have been sliced cheese. Whenever Joseph saw Steve, no matter where we might be, he would pull over, shout an excited greeting, then put his Elvis CD on at full blast. That done, he would then begin dancing alongside his taxi, which no one appeared to find unusual in any way. We could have been at the ferry terminal or having a coffee at the market square in Victoria; it made no difference. We would hear a cry of elation, see a lot of waving by a large, hairy arm, then hear *Hound Dog, Jailhouse Rock* or similar blaring out of the taxi, with Joseph dancing away oblivious to his surroundings.

"See?" he would cheer. "I play Elvis for you! All the time, I am playing Elvis."

Steve and I would wave back in a small, subdued manner, while keeping our heads down and smiling apologetically at startled passers-by. Joseph continually promised that he would come and see us sing sometime and one night he made good on his promise.

On the night in question, we had been singing at *The Captain's Table* in Xlendi and who should enter but Joseph accompanied by three people. I nodded my head in the direction of the door and Steve smiled on seeing him. Joseph got a drink and threw himself wholeheartedly into the evening. He danced and sweated, drink in hand, waving to Steve all the time.

"I said I would come," he said with great relish.

After about half an hour of exuberant gyrations, Joseph was almost spent. His friends did not seem to share his enthusiasm. They had remained seated somewhat indifferently without even getting a drink. Eventually, Joseph mopped up his brow, went over to Steve, took a deep breath and said:

"I've enjoyed it, but now I must go. These people have to get the ferry."

Steve stared in disbelief. Joseph's 'friends' were actually paying customers who had been brought reluctantly and involuntarily to the show. Only in Gozo, folks! Only in Gozo.

As I sat on the wall looking down on the beautiful vista before me, I chuckled as I recalled our day out on the open top bus which is one of the main tourist attractions on the island. When we had first arrived there, we had taken good advice and invested 15 euros each to tour the island on the bus, which came complete with audio commentary. It had proved a really brilliant way to see the whole island, stopping off where we wanted and hopping back on an hour or so later when our explorations were completed. On the way back, the bus had made its way slowly down the hill into Marsalforn from the hilltop village of Xagħra. As it did so, we approached a construction team who were working on a block of flats. With some consternation, I noticed that they were in the process of swinging a load of concrete blocks high overhead by crane. You did not need to be a mathematical genius to calculate that we would pass right underneath as the blocks were overhead. Steve had seen it too.

"Well, this should be interesting," he said.

The driver and the construction crew both seemed to appreciate the situation at the same time. The bus ground to a halt, accompanied by a lot of shouting and gesticulating. The only trouble was that we were now immediately underneath the swinging load, which hung precariously above our heads. It was too much for one tourist who uttered a cry of disbelief, raced down the stairs and leapt off. The rest of us watched in fascination and no one, apart from the unfortunate tourist who bolted, seemed to consider the situation in any way dangerous or worrisome. The workmen waved at us cheerily and I managed to photograph the scene, bearing in mind that we could easily need proof for an insurance claim.

At that moment, the inevitable happened. The pallet which had been carrying the blocks gave way to its excessive load. A four-feet-long piece of 2" x 4" wood broke off and hurtled towards the bus. We all envied the tourist who had managed to escape and I wondered vaguely if he had been psychic. The offending projectile descended at high velocity and scraped right down the side of the bus, thankfully avoiding all the passengers, but only just. Steve and I exchanged looks of utter amazement and I realised that I was holding my breath. We looked up to see the builder smiling and waving to us as if nothing happened. The bus driver took the same view and went on his merry way. There was no need to make a big fuss. It was just another day in Gozo.

Freya and Steve during a performance

CHAPTER 16

Having relocated to Gozo from the UK, our intention was to work there as entertainers – something Steve had been doing for most of his life, while I had been singing professionally for four years. Steve had been a professional session drummer since his teens and played all over the world. He also played guitar and keyboard, and wrote music and lyrics.

Steve had fallen into singing by accident. He was at a recording session playing his drums once, when he was asked to stand in as a backing singer due to the regular singer being unwell. Steve had acquiesced to that request, while protesting that he was a musician, not a singer. As he sang, in fact, he could see people smiling.

"That bad?" he asked, only to be told to listen to the playback.

The unanimous opinion was that he sounded uncannily like Elvis Presley and so his singing career was born. Steve needed no agent and he did not advertise. His reputation as an Elvis performer was pretty much legendary and he continued working through word of mouth. On the one hand, Steve was in demand at weddings and private functions, and people adored him. On the other hand, I was unknown, untested and starting from scratch. With huge support from Steve, I attended auditions and, before long, I had three agents: one in the North, one on the East Coast and another one further South. We were, in short, busy.

Travelling around the country as entertainers brought its fair share of laughs. One club that I shall always remember was a large, well-maintained establishment in Nottingham. It had a good membership and was well attended. It was a solo gig for me and I was looking forward to it.

"Full house," grinned Steve, peeping through the curtains as I put on make-up and squeezed my body into a sparkly dress. "Off you go," he encouraged with a wink.

And off I went. I bounded onto the stage with my usual enthusiasm and zest for the newfound career I loved so much. Now, as a rule, after the opening song, you can gauge what kind of a night you are going to have. Most places, out of politeness if nothing else, will applaud even if your songs are not to their taste. I sing a lot of 60's and 70's music, along with rock-and-roll and country music. It generally goes down well with older audiences in the clubs as it is what they knew and grew up with. Also as a rule, I was pretty well received and to be rebooked for three months' time was the norm. However, that particular night was going to be hard work. No one clapped, no one moved. Nothing.

I pressed on, song after song. Nothing. They were all watching closely, but seemed to be what we commonly refer to as "dead from the neck up." I persevered, grimacing at Steve who sat cueing up my songs. He shrugged his shoulders in bewilderment and the end of the first set could not come fast enough.

"They hate me," I said anxiously as I came off.

"They don't hate you," said Steve, doing his best to cheer me up. "They're just, well, quiet."

"No, they hate me," I lamented. "Oh, God! That was such hard work, I don't want to go back on. Mind you, they'll probably pay me off and tell me to leave after that first spot. It was a disaster," I continued, unabated.

"They won't pay you off, don't be silly," soothed Steve.

He was right. They did not pay me off and I had to go on and do it all again. The second spot was as bad as the first. I gave up on the small talk and just concentrated on singing and getting it over and done with. I would not be asked back there, that was for sure. I was already mentally ringing my agent and telling him not to send me there again.

Finally, it was time for the third and last spot. I decided to give it my all and opened with *Whole Lotta Shakin Goin On*. I sprang onto the stage in my short, sequined dress, which one very good friend had described as my "barely legal dress," high heels, shaking my booty and belting it out. I looked into the audience: it was like a scene from night of the living dead. Not one single person was so much as tapping their foot or lifting a finger to tap a table. It was too much. I started laughing – and I mean laughing. Throwing caution to the wind, I stopped singing and said:

"Oh, come ON! Whole lotta shakin and no one's moving. Jeez!"

Steve looked at me in alarm and mouthed, "What ARE you doing?"

I shrugged.

"Start it again, would you, please?" I asked as the laughter dried up in my mouth.

And so it went on, right up to the bitter end. Not one shred of acknowledgement, not one single hand clap. Nothing. I despaired, but reached the glaring conclusion that they did, in fact, hate me.

Not a moment too soon, it was over and we could pack up and leave – and for me, the sooner, the better. As we were packing, I noticed a little old man in a flat cap sidling up to the stage. He was bent and grizzled, and he beckoned to me.

"Oh, God!" I said to Steve. "Here we go. He's going to tell me how bad I was."

I forced a bright smile and went over to the man. I strained to hear him from the stage and, in the end, had to kneel down and put my ear close to his mouth.

"We've ad a reet good night, lass," he wheezed, asthmatically. "You're a proper, good turn," he continued, heaping praise onto me.

I shook my head in disbelief.

"Really?" I said in amazement. "I didn't think I went down too well."

"Nay, lass. You were a top act," finished the little man as he tottered off.

"Well, I never!" I exclaimed, turning to Steve. "Did you hear that?"

"No. What did he say?" asked Steve, busy with the task of wire winding.

"Well, he liked me so I got one of them, I guess."

I smiled as I went to help pack up.

"You've got another one," said Steve, nodding his head towards the front of the stage.

And the strange scene was repeated as another flat-capped gentleman whispered his gratitude up to me.

"Well done, lass. It's been a good night," he croaked. "One to remember. You'll be asked back, no doubt."

And off he went. That process continued as, one by one, people approached the stage and said that they had enjoyed a good night. Some even went so far as to grip my hand in silent solidarity. I was mystified. Finally, a wizened gnome of a man approached the stage and considered me out of his rheumy, old eyes. I went through the same routine of kneeling down to hear what he had to say. He drew himself up importantly before declaring with some seriousness:

"I'm t'club secretary ere and you've been one of the best artistes we've ad."

"Well, thank you," I offered. "I really didn't think I'd gone down too well. I mean, no one clapped at all."

The old man studied me for a moment then solemnly said, "Lass, if bloody Frank Sinatra sang ere, these miserable buggers wouldn't clap."

And with that he was gone. He had made my night and I beamed all the way home. Nevertheless, when my agent rang to tell me that they wanted to book me again, I was lightning fast in my response. It was a polite, but firm, no thank you.

When we had made the move to Gozo, we knew that rates of pay for entertainment were less than in the UK. However, we had no idea how big a difference there was. To our dismay, we discovered that, on average, it was about half. As our options for singing in Gozo were more limited, Steve and I visited Malta within a week of our arrival to meet with owners and managers of hotels, bars and restaurants who could be interested in us providing entertainment at their places. We immediately secured work in the tourist area of Qawra and managed to successfully negotiate the prices *up*, but it was still nowhere near what we had been getting in the UK. But then it was not the UK, so it was no use complaining about it.

Our first gig in Malta was a joint one in Qawra. We played to a packed, enthusiastic house and were told that people were not used to our style of entertainment. When we sang, we engaged the audience and moved around among them. Steve is especially skilled at that and always generates a fantastic atmosphere. After that show, we were both offered the opportunity to have our own residency at the place, one of us on Saturday night and the other on Sunday. We agreed.

Other work followed and soon we had a reasonable following not only of locals, but of expats who were regular visitors to the island, staying for the whole of January and February to escape the UK winters. Prices at some of the hotels in Malta were so reasonable that it worked out cheaper for them to live there for 2 months, than to stay in the UK, paying high fuel bills and coping with the weather. The bar owners soon caught onto the fact that we brought paying customers with us, so before we knew it, we were singing in Malta five nights a week. That was okay, but tiring and very time consuming to the point that we considered moving to Malta full time.

Singing in Malta, as opposed to Gozo, brought a host of new challenges. For a start, we had to get the ferry for the 25-minute sailing, then make a 40-minute journey on the other side, to the actual venue. The trip on the ferry was nothing less than entertaining in itself. Passengers would wander on and off the ferry at the same time, and through the same entrance as the cars and the lorries. We would marvel at the total lack of health and safety, and watch in disbelief as people dodged and sidestepped in their efforts to board. Cars would be swerving to miss them and emergency stops were commonplace. Getting off the ferry was even worse. As soon as the ferry door started to open, the drivers would start blasting their horns impatiently. No one could go anywhere as the doors were not yet fully down. It made no difference, however. The cacophony of noise was a regular feature of ferry travel between Malta and Gozo (I am pleased to say that things have now improved and passengers do not board with vehicles any more). Once off the ferry and onto the roads, we had the ongoing problem of flat tyres. The roads over in Malta are bumpy and full of potholes, and no matter how carefully you drive, flat tyres seem to be the norm. I lost count of the number of times we went out of a gig, only for Steve to have to roll up his sleeves and change a tyre.

One place we had visited in search of work was owned by a Maltese guy whom I shall call Mario. He had clearly been in the business for many years and had a kind of crispy, weathered look about him. His bar was dark and dingy, but could seat a fair few people, with an additional area outside. He wanted to know if we could provide entertainment for New Year's Eve. We said that we could and gave him what we felt was a fair price, but on hearing our suggested rate, Mario acquired a pallor and clutched at his forehead.

"It's too much!" he exclaimed, dramatically.

By now, Steve and I had got wise to that tactic. It was always "too much." If we said 10 euros, no doubt it would still have been too much, but we were determined not to commit to New Year's Eve for a pittance.

"Well, that's what we charge for New Year's Eve," explained Steve, pleasantly.

Mario took on the appearance of a man having a small stroke. He held his hand to his chest and gasped.

"No, no. It's too much!"

"Okay," said Steve. "No worries. Thanks for your time."

And we made to walk off.

"Wait," came the strangled response as Mario clung to life. "OKAY. I will pay it . . . . . but it's too much!"

We shook hands on the deal, but could hear Mario muttering as we left:

"I'm paying too high a price. I'm being robbed."

New Year's Eve came around soon enough. Mario's place was packed to capacity, the atmosphere was good and away we went. After my first spot, I went, as is my custom, to change into another costume. Steve put some backing music on, so that the party atmosphere continued. However, Mario followed me.

"Where are you going?" he enquired, anxiously.

"Oh, I'm just going to get a quick change," I explained. "Don't worry, I'll be back on in 10 minutes."

Mario looked aghast upon hearing that news.

"No, no, no!" he protested, assuming the look of a man who had been told he had only minutes to live. "Keep it going, keep it going," he urged.

I looked startled at Mario.

"We have to take a break. We're going to be here for about six hours, we have to take a break. And Steve is playing music," I replied.

Mario dramatically rolled his eyes.

"I'm paying a high price," he complained. "You must keep it going."

I sighed.

"I think you better talk to Steve," I replied.

"Did he say anything to you? I need to get going again, he's pretty anxious," I said to Steve when I returned from getting changed.

Steve raised one eyebrow and I was immediately jealous, wishing I could do that. It was so Roger Moore.

"Yes," Steve replied laconically, while pouring me a coffee from the flask we had with us. "He did say something."

Steve continued busying himself with setting up the equipment for the second spot. I was intrigued.

"Well, what'd he say?" I asked.

Again, the eyebrow was up.

"I explained to him the way things are done," Steve continued. "He now understands how the night will proceed."

Mario never asked again, but stood sulkily behind his bar. However, he stared at us continually and I could hear his mental urgings to *keep it going*.

He had no reason to complain. We sang from 8.00pm until 2.30am and he never so much as offered us a drink. *Too much, indeed!* Good job we had a flask with us.

We had further problems with Mario down the line. He pestered us for weeks to return back and sing at his place. Eventually, we agreed, but he had not changed. He was as stressed and demanding as ever. As we were leaving, he tried to book us again. We stalled, saying that we would ring him. He then made a fatal error.

Mario said, "You sing for me, yes? I have you every Friday. I do not want to see you singing in any other places in Qawra!"

My mouth dropped open at the audacity of what had he just said and I inhaled sharply. Steve's mouth set into a thin line and his eyes narrowed. He leaned in towards Mario and stared at him for a dangerous length of time.

"What did you just say to me?" Steve asked, darkly.

His blood pressure was rising and his hands were opening and closing in that pre-bar fight way. Recognising the primeval look on Steve's face and the inevitable way it would progress if he pressed his point, Mario mumbled something incomprehensible.

The man added quickly, "Ring me, ring me."

Then he slunk off behind his bar. Needless to say, we did not return.

However, we had not heard the last of Mario. We had been singing regularly in another venue close to his and one night got a call from the owner. She was highly agitated and asked if we were still singing at her place that night. I reassured her that we were. She went on to tell me that Mario had a poster up, advertising us for that night at his place. I said that we were definitely not singing at his place – not now, not ever. She then said that he had done it on purpose, to make people think that we were singing there and not at her place. I could not believe my ears and relayed the information to Steve.

When we arrived at the place we were booked to sing, Steve set up all the equipment and did the sound check. Then he quietly put on his coat and gloves – fighting gloves, no less.

"Back soon," he said without further explanation.

I instantly knew where he had gone: right down to do further explaining with our 'friend' around the corner. The incident was not repeated and that was the last we heard of Mario.

Steve and I consider ourselves professional entertainers. It does not matter if the venue is big or small. We give 100% of ourselves in effort and presentation, and strive to do the best we can. When we performed in Malta, we enjoyed the support of genuine people and usually sang to a packed audience who would ask us where we were going to be next. Sad to say, many owners of the places where we performed were jaded by years of tourists and ever-increasing costs. Bar owners were constantly trying to lower the price they paid to the likes of us.

There were literally dozens of venues in Qawra and the surrounding area, most of which provided entertainment seven nights a week in all seasons. Competition between the venues was fierce and we soon realised that our professionalism was not necessarily appreciated. Our new good friend, Manwel, had become our manager and proved to be a huge asset. One of his particular talents was producing high quality posters for the venues. He would be sure to email them to the owner in good time for the coming gig. Time after time, however, we would arrive to find that they had not bothered to print off the poster and advertise properly, but had simply scrawled out our names in chalk on the blackboard outside. More often than not, they misspelled our names and one night I was even given an unwanted gender change and billed as a man! We were fast becoming disillusioned, but we stuck with it as we had gone there to sing – and sing we did.

During the winter months of January and early February, the ferries were quiet and for a while, singing was pretty uneventful and routine. We would normally leave the house at around 6.30pm to catch the 7.00pm ferry, which got us to the gig in good time. One day, however, we tootled down, only to find that there were hundreds of cars in a long snake of a queue. We initially thought that there had been an accident. After all, Gozo was not known for traffic jams; they barely even had traffic lights. Of course, we missed our planned ferry and watched anxiously as the cars lined up to get onto the next one. We missed that one too and had to ring the venue, to explain that we would be terribly late that night.

We then discovered that many visitors to Gozo were Maltese people who had a second home on the small island. They went over on weekends and from around February, the queues for the ferry to Malta would start forming at around 4.00pm as the people left to return home. That gave us a real dilemma. In order to be on time, we needed to be in the queue at around 5.00pm. It not only meant leaving Ollie on his own way too long, but also made it an extremely long evening for us. Most places expected us to sing from 8.00pm until midnight, which meant that we had to race to catch the ferry back, which left at around 1.00am. If we missed that ferry, which we did several times, we had to just sit at the terminal until 2.30am. When we calculated the hours we were out and divided them by the amount of money we were actually getting, minus the ferry fare and the fuel costs, we came to one glaring conclusion: with the best will in the world, it was simply not worth it. By March, we had stopped singing in Malta.

It was in the midst of all of the above that I sat one day trying to make our meagre earnings stretch to pay the water and electricity bills, as well as the phone bill, gas bill, petrol and food.

"I give in," I declared in defeat. "This is not why we came here: to be scratching around for 10 euros here and 10 euros there. I'm freezing cold, living in constant damp and it's still only March. Who on earth told us that Malta had a lovely winter climate?" I lamented.

Steve could only nod in agreement. Thus it was that we reached the reluctant and undesirable decision that I would return to the UK, to boost our depleted savings by re-entering the workforce. As a freelance consultant to the local government over in the UK, my earning potential was pretty good and I would be able to return to Gozo before the summer. Steve would have to remain in Gozo as now at 20 years old, we were not prepared to leave Ollie with anyone. We were both going to be on our own.

It felt like a retrograde step and if I am to be open and honest, a complete failure, but as we had just about run out of savings, we had no other viable options. We were back to square one and at that point, the grass did not seem so green. I was returning back to the UK.

CHAPTER 17

O h, the misfortune of having to return to the UK! We had got used to pleasing ourselves and going for a coffee whenever we felt like it. Steve and I had become accustomed to long, leisurely walks by the sea, visiting various places of beauty and generally behaving as if we had retired – which we most certainly had not. Without too much effort, I secured work in the Isle of Man. That was as good as I could have hoped for as my very best friend, Heather, lived there, which if I am to be honest was the only attraction for my going there. Like many people, I hate travelling. Let me elaborate.

I hate travelling when it does not involve a sun-drenched holiday, complete with five-star, luxury hotel; cocktails and a white, sandy beach at the other end. To go to the Isle of Man, best friend aside, did not fill me with overwhelming joy. The other thing I particularly hate is the whole travelling experience of actually getting to your destination, which for me would involve:

1. Trip to the ferry – a mere 10 minutes;
2. Taxi to the airport – one hour;
3. Long wait for flight – three hours;
4. Flight to Manchester – three hours, 20 minutes;
5. Long wait for connecting flight – an unbelievable five hours;
6. Flight to Isle of Man – 35 minutes;
7. Trip from the airport to new digs – thankfully, with best friend; no time at all.

Anyway, you get the idea. And so it was that I embarked on my epic journey. To say that I was sad was the understatement of the century. Steve and I are soul mates and do not do well when we are apart from each other. We said our goodbyes at the ferry terminal. I cried and Steve got something in his eye. I was off.

The annoyances began almost immediately as once I disembarked in Malta, there was no sign of my pre-booked taxi. I waited a few minutes, then in my usual obsessive-compulsive manner, had to ring to see what was happening.

"He's on his way," soothed the voice on the phone. "There's been an accident in Mellieħa which has held him up, but he's on his way now," she continued by way of explanation.

Ten minutes later, the taxi duly arrived.

"Morning," I said as cheerfully as I could muster under the circumstances. "Was it a bad accident?" I enquired once inside.

"Accident?" asked the driver in complete ignorance of the lie which now became apparent. "There is no accident," he said shaking his head.

And off we went. Taxi companies, it seems, are the same the world over.

I can think of fewer things which bore me as much as waiting at an airport. Of course, my inability to sit still for more than five seconds does not help. Steve likens me to a wasp on speed as I constantly have to get up and down, wander around, check and recheck our passports and boarding passes, and generally behave annoyingly. When we are together, we usually book into the airport lounge, which I had not bothered to do on my own. I was, therefore, left to wander the duty-free shops, wistfully wishing I could buy every product in there.

It was finally time to go through airport security and I had paid for fast tracking. Try as I might to fight it, this has always evoked feelings of superiority. So I sailed past the other, less well organised holiday makers, while keeping an anxious and watchful eye on the other queue to ensure that it was not moving as fast as mine. It was not so much that I had paid for my queue to go faster; I was paying for them to go slower.

I was ready for the security checkpoint. Laptop? Already out of my bag and ready for inspection. Gels, liquids? Nope, all in the hold luggage.

Valuables? All in the little plastic box, ready to go. I looked around and could only shake my head in despair and disapproval. There were always people who were left fumbling to get their laptops out of their bags at the last minute and men looking amazed when asked to remove their belts. *Was it not crystal clear from the multiple signs what was required?* I sighed, certain in the knowledge that the staff must value a seasoned traveller such as myself who was ready to be screened without a fuss.

I passed through the metal detectors, smiling in a knowing way to the woman at the other side. I conveyed my silent understanding of her frustration at the disorderly, haphazard passengers behind me and stepped confidently through.

Beep, Beep, Beep, said the scanners. *What was that? It could not be me, could it?!* The woman called me over. *Oh, the shame of it!* I was being patted down. I spluttered and stammered.

"But, but, I've not got anything on me," I began. "I took it all out and I've not got a belt on or anything. I can't understand this," I continued in huge embarrassment.

The woman looked at me accusingly.

"What's this in your pocket?" she asked, suspiciously.

I reached into my pocket and, to my horror, discovered about 45 cents in loose change that I had got when buying a pack of chewing gum. I had stuck them in my pocket and forgotten all about them. I had to slink back and put them in a plastic box, and start all over again. The other passengers sighed collectively in disbelief and shook their heads. *Were the signs not clear?* There was always one. I could imagine the staff behind the one-way glass, high fiving each other as they finally caught me out.

Eventually, we were called for boarding. I had not bothered to book a seat as I was on my own and it did not really matter where I sat. I had waited until the last minute to board and found that a man-and-wife couple had sat on the front row, but sneakily sat in the aisle and window seat, leaving the middle seat unoccupied. I could see right through their ploy. They hoped no one would sit there, leaving them with the entire front row to spread out and relax. Of course, I ruined their plans.

Innocently, I started, "Is anyone sitting here?" indicating the middle seat.

The couple had cunningly placed their newspaper on it, in the hope that it would make it look occupied. At my question, therefore, they glowered and exchanged glances which said:

"Damn, we didn't think anyone would sit here."

Obviously, they did not want me, like some unwelcome weed in their midst, so the woman begrudgingly moved to the middle to sit beside her husband. Result! I had the front aisle seat at no cost. *Ha! Something had gone to plan . . . . . Oh, hang on, they're changing places! She's unhappy with her middle seat and has insisted on being by the window.* It was at that point I realised that the man was not only huge, but hairy beyond belief and resembled a cross between a hippopotamus and Bigfoot. He was also rudely overflowing into my seat in what I was certain was a counter tactic to my initial query. I, therefore, had to endure three hours and 20 minutes of trying to make myself as small as I possible, while trying not to sigh loudly and pointedly.

Restraint is not my strong point and I think I let a few, deep sighs escape, and maybe a pointed look or two as well. The man hogged the arm of the seat and the surplus fat from his back encroached sweatily into my personal space in a highly irritating manner. I resigned myself to an uncomfortable and cramped journey, but consoled myself with the amount of legroom I had in front of me. That victory was minor and short lived, however, as I realised that I now had to tolerate the endless streams of people who needed to use the bathroom. *Good God!* They had weaker bladders than mine, which was saying something. As they queued, they would jostle into me, banging my head, arm or right leg, which I had to position somewhat in the aisle due to Bigfoot man to my left. It brought to my mind the scene in the film *Airplane* where they all line up to slap the hysterical passenger. I was sure that one by one, everyone was having a go at me. I made a mental note to book a seat next time and definitely not the front aisle seat, that was for sure.

I arrived in the UK with aching jaws from the amount of teeth grinding I had done. To add insult to injury, I now had an unbelievable five-hour wait for my 35-minute flight to the Isle of Man. I looked for a quiet place to sit and read my book, and found one in an unoccupied corner. As it was excessively early to check in my bags, I arranged them around me in a kind of antisocial barricade, got my book out and settled in for the duration. Naturally, 10 minutes later I was bored and wanted a coffee. To get one, I would have to surrender my quiet seat and risk losing it, but my need for a coffee overwhelmed me and with great reluctance, I dragged my bags across to the café and ordered a coffee. On hearing that my order would require me to part with £4, I tried not to:

1. Laugh;
2. Cry;
3. Shout, "What??! Are you kidding me? £4 for a coffee?"
4. Give unsolicited advice as to what a cup of coffee would cost me back in Gozo (*one euro*);
5. Give a short lecture on how much it actually cost to produce said cup of coffee.

I restrained myself and paid up. Then I spied a rather nice-looking baguette, but on being told that it would cost me £6.50, I decided to starve on principal. I returned hurriedly to my seat, which was not easy with two bags and a cup of scalding coffee, but I managed it. To my dismay, a man had sat down in my quiet corner, but not in my actual chair. I weighed up the options. He was on his own and far enough away for me to be able to continue in my antisocial world. So I rearranged my baggage fortifications and resumed my seat – a decision I soon came to regret. Within minutes, the rest of the man's startlingly huge family arrived to join him.

"Come on, come on," he trilled in an unmistakeable Irish brogue. "Sure now, I've saved you all a seat here, so I have," he called loudly across the hallway.

"Daddy!" called a young girl on seeing him.

"Daddy," echoed an indeterminate number of other small children with equal enthusiasm as they all converged on what had been my quiet corner.

"Ah, Michael, there you are," called the legion of adults following the children.

I realised that I was holding my breath as I watched in disbelief. *How could one man have such a large family? Had he no restraint?* Chairs were dragged from all directions as the family made themselves comfortable. There was one chair left opposite me and on which, for a moment, I considered putting up my feet. However, the family's flame-haired matriarch beat me to it.

"Can I take this chair, me darlin'?" she asked, pleasantly.

I forced a smile, pretended that I had only just noticed her and her unrestrained brood, and said winningly, "Why, of course."

Inwardly, I was horrified. The airport was now very busy and I had few other seating choices. I was also trapped in my previously quiet corner by the prodigious family who were eying my chair longingly as despite commandeering every available seat, they were still short by three and having to make do with children on knees. I knew that if I so much as shifted my weight, they would whip it from under me. No, I was staying put.

There then followed a scene of complete chaos as Auntie Sinead tried to take an order for food. I wanted to shout a warning about the cost of such an unwise decision, but it was too late. Two of the younger members of the family had been dispatched to the café and returned a very long time later with trays of food and beverages. A lot had been spilled on the return journey, which provoked a great deal of scolding from the women. I had little doubt that Michael would end up with no change out of 100 quid.

My decision to stay put was short-lived. As fortified no doubt by his pint of overpriced *Guinness*, Uncle Patrick produced an harmonica and to my great consternation, began belting out a tune. The family were unable to curb their enthusiasm and as one voice began singing the unmistakeable *Wild Rover*. Auntie Coleen led, with Auntie Bridget and Uncle Joseph putting in a spirited harmony.

"Ah, come on, children," encouraged Michael.

They needed no second asking and all joined in with uninhibited abandon.

"That's the way," warbled Michael with excessive jolliness, unmistakeably proud of his musical brood.

That was it! I stood up to move, which had the same unfortunate effect of a movie director shouting, "Cut." The singing was immediately terminated and the entire family fixed me with a penetrating gaze. I swear that even the baby managed an unblinking stare.

"You're not leaving on account of us, are you, missus?" asked Uncle Finbar, genuinely concerned.

"No, no, no, no, no," I replied too many times. "Not at all," I lied. "No, I just need to go and see if my plane's boarding yet."

"Ah, well, okay. We may as well use your chair if you're off then," said Auntie Shauna.

And she proceeded to whip it out from under me as I had known all along that she would at the slightest chance.

I was now reduced to wandering around the airport like some forsaken refugee. I realised that I needed to go to the *Ladies*, which was no small task with two large bags in tow. I applied myself to solving the problem and wondered if I could sneak in and out of the toilets for the disabled without being detected. Like many people born under the sign of Capricorn, I have a puritanical streak of honesty running through the middle of me like the lettering in Blackpool Rock. I found it almost impossible to even think about using the toilets for the disabled. After all, I am not disabled. However, I knew that I had no chance of getting into the regular toilets with my bags – not if I wanted to shut the door. So I reluctantly decided to use one of those toilets. I did give a brief thought to adopting an ailment in order to justify myself if challenged, but unable to come up with anything credible, I abandoned my scruples and went in. When I emerged a few minutes later, I was embarrassed to discover someone waiting in a wheelchair.

"Those toilets are for disabled use, you know," said the woman who was, quite rightly, offended.

I opened my mouth to explain, but no words came out. *Busted!* I decided to give up on my exceedingly bad idea not to go into the airport lounge. It seemed the only way to achieve the peace and quiet I craved. It was also an excuse to eat and drink my own bodyweight if I so desired. I stumped up the fee and sank down into a comfortable leather chair in a genuinely quiet corner, free from mad Irish families who sang *Wild Rover* and stole your chair as soon as your back was turned. Having surveyed the food on offer, I decided that I would go for the cheese and the crackers as I did not like the other selections. I piled my plate up with the tiny, doll-like packets and retreated to have my own little picnic in the corner. I allowed myself one gin and tonic, knowing full well that if I had any more it was highly likely that I would fall heavily asleep and miss my connecting flight.

Within minutes, my reverie was disrupted by the unmistakeable sound of a video game being played too loudly. I sat bolt upright, scanning anxiously for the Irish family. *Had they followed me in??* What I saw was a small boy of about eight years of age on the computer. He was engrossed in playing a game and oblivious to my disapproving looks. *That would absolutely not do! Why was there even a child in there?* I got up and walked around the room, trying to work out whom his parents were. However, I gave up as I feared that I was wasting perfectly good, indignant glares on innocent bystanders. Instead, I walked past the child.

"Turn it down," I hissed.

To my great surprise, he did. Finally and not a moment too soon, my flight to the Isle of Man was boarding. It was a tiny little plane which hardly looked sturdy enough for the task, but 35 minutes later I was touching down. I had arrived full circle, from one small island to another. For the first time since leaving Steve, I felt a tinge of happiness as I saw my friend, Heather, waiting for me. She was waving and smiling.

I had arrived.

Sunset in Gozo

CHAPTER 18

The Proposal

With the invaluable support of my friend, we made it to the allocated digs which were to be my temporary home for six weeks. My first impression of that old nurse's home was one of panic: it had the look and feel of a 1950's institution. Brick built, flat front, flat roof, austere, impersonal and without any character whatsoever. I hated it immediately. As we made our way up the stairs to the first floor, I surveyed the interior with dismay. It was tired, worn and old, and certainly not what I had in mind when I agreed to the contract. It even smelled like an institution and just when I thought it could not get any worse, I arrived at what was to be my room.

Heather and I stood in the doorway, blinking in silence. Lino floor, one set of drawers, one single bed, one sink and one chair; that was it. The heating was turned up to volcanic, making it almost impossible to breathe. The bathroom was a shared one down the hall. The other dozens of rooms were occupied by other social workers, nurses and doctors. I turned to Heather.

"There's no way I'm staying here," I said, simply.

My friend agreed and reassured me that she would help me to find alternative accommodation, but there was nothing to be done for that night so I had to accept my lot and try settling in. Heather hugged me and left. I experienced an overwhelming rush of loneliness. I missed Steve very much, but without any internet connection I was unable to do anything other than text him to say that I had arrived safely. He rang me up immediately, which in my emotional and tired state provoked an outburst of tears. Talking to him made me even more homesick and once I hung up, sleep was impossible. The heat was ridiculous, but I dared not open a window for fear of intruders. I lay on the tiny bed and allowed my mind to wander back in escape.

~ ~ ~ ~ ~

Steve and I had been together for four years, having met when I went to watch him perform in the UK on that fateful day in 2005. It really was love at first sight for both of us. Once we had both divorced our previous partners, the dust finally settled and we decided to get engaged. I had chosen a beautiful ruby and diamond ring, but was not permitted to wear it until Steve officially proposed to me. That was so exciting for me, having been previously married to someone whose idea of a romantic night out was a two-for-one meal at *Weatherspoon's!* I had no idea when Steve intended to propose. I just knew it was imminent.

It was the festive season of 2008 and we were busy with our UK singing engagements. We had been booked to perform together at a lively pub on New Year's Eve, where we had sung the previous year and it had been a really brilliant night. It was extremely busy and everyone was in party mood, enjoying themselves. Time reached 11:55pm and Steve asked for silence, saying that he had something very important to disclose. A hush descended over the crowd and he pulled out my ring. I was completely taken aback. Despite knowing that he would propose to me at some point, I did not see it coming. In the ensuing silence, I heard a woman tearfully say:

"Oh, he's going to propose to her."

And he did. Steve got down on one knee to the *Ooohs* and *Aaahs* of the people watching and said my name . . . . . that was all he managed to say. Before any more words could come out of his mouth, I shouted:

"YES! YES! YES!" much to the amusement of the people in the pub.

Steve patiently explained that he had not yet asked me anything and that I did not know what he was going to say. He finally got a word in edgeways and asked me to marry him. It was a no-brainer and anyway, I had already agreed before he asked. From nowhere, someone produced a massive bottle of champagne for us and to this day, I have no idea from where they got it.

Thus it was that Steve and I became engaged. I wore my ring with so much pride and still do. I had never previously had an engagement ring – *Weatherspoon's*, remember? – and I still felt like a love-struck teenager. We decided that we would love to get married in Hawaii, but it was going to be hugely expensive and seemed a distant dream. We did not set a date, but carried on with life, enjoying each other's company.

~ ~ ~ ~ ~

I never imagined that we would have to live apart so soon after moving to our dream destination of Gozo. Yet here I was, alone and miserable, in little more than an overheated prison cell, about to begin a new job in the morning. Exhaustion finally got the better of me and I settled into a fitful sleep, dreaming of crystal clear waters, blue lagoons and Steve.

On the bright side, being in the Isle of Man meant that Heather and I could talk weddings – wonderful. I began to look for a totally unconventional wedding dress and one day, as I wandered around during lunch break, I spotted what I thought was *the one*. The dress was in a small boutique in Douglas and looked like it might have belonged to Jessica Rabbit. It was a clingy, low cut, split-sided beauty of a dress – oh, and it was turquoise. I loved it from the moment I saw it and rushed in to try it on. *Hmmm, a tad snug.* I knew that a strict diet would be on the cards. I asked the staff to put the dress to one side for me until Heather could see it and give me her opinion, which I knew would be brutally honest.

On Saturday, we both went back to the shop so that I could show her the dress. I put it on and nervously emerged from the changing room.

"Well?" I asked, "What do you think?"

Then I asked the question women have undoubtedly been asking since the Stone Age.

"Do I look fat?"

Heather surveyed me with a critical eye and smiled.

"I expected nothing less. It's very 'you,'" she replied.

That made us both laugh. Heather then said that I would, indeed, need to lose weight. See? I told you she would be brutally honest! Heather agreed, however, that the dress was perfect for me and I went back to change, handing her the dress through the curtain. When I emerged again, my friend was at the counter putting her credit card away.

"Err, what just happened here?" I asked with suspicion as I joined her.

Then my dear friend – my lovely, generous, wonderful best friend – replied, "If your mum was still here, she'd be buying this for you. You don't have your mum now, so this is my gift to you."

I burst into tears and was quickly joined by Heather as we hugged. Next thing we knew, the girl in the shop was also in tears.

"Oh, that's so lovely! She bought her the dress!" said the girl.

The male assistant came over to ask what was going on and when he heard about it, he too began to cry. There was not one dry eye in the whole shop. I will be eternally grateful to my friend for that dress: not just for the act of unselfish generosity, but for the gesture and the sentiment behind it. Thank you, my friend!

Although I now had my lovely wedding dress, I was still fretting as we had not set the date for our wedding and more importantly, we did not even have a venue. But one night, when Steve and I were talking on Skype, he made a simple announcement:

"26th October: that's when we're getting married. 26th October; that's that."

So that was, indeed, that. The date was set for our wedding and I was abuzz with excitement. Through the internet, I got shoes to match for my dress and Steve bought me some stunning jewellery to compliment the said dress, although he had not yet seen it and would not do so until the day. I bought a tiara, but as I could not find one in turquoise, I painted some of the stones with turquoise nail varnish – I tell you, it worked. We agreed that the wedding colours would be turquoise and white, with Steve getting married in a white suit.

Then I asked Steve if he had managed to go into Victoria – the capital of Gozo – to organise the wedding date with the Registry Office there. Steve looked rather bemused and said that he thought it was arranged. When I asked what he meant by that, he told me that he had been to visit and explained that we wanted to get married on the 26th October. The woman in charge had simply stood up, walked over to a calendar on the wall and circled the date in pencil. Then she returned to her seat.

"There!" she exclaimed in a satisfied way.

I was aghast.

"That's IT?" I asked in disbelief. "No booking it into a computer or even into a diary? Just a circle in pencil on a wall calendar?"

Steve shrugged.

"Well, yes. That's all that seemed necessary."

And it was.

Steve and Freya during another performance

CHAPTER 19

The Unexpected

Thankfully, time passed quickly in the Isle of Man. After the initial accommodation nightmare, Heather managed to locate a stunning, one bedroom flat on the promenade in Douglas, which made the experience bearable and I stayed there for the remainder of my visit. My work soon came to an end and I was free to return to my beloved Gozo to continue planning our wedding.

The one nagging issue was still the venue, which was yet to be decided. One day, while Steve and I were still exploring the area, we went for a walk in the village of Xagħra (pronounced Shara). We parked in the square up by the huge church and wandered off in no particular direction. It was a beautiful, sunny day and we gravitated towards the sea views over Marsalforn. Eventually as always, I needed the *Ladies* and as we continued our walk, we came across a hotel named *Cornucopia*.

"I'm sure they'd let me use the loo," I told Steve, "especially if we have a coffee here."

Little did we know what an opportunistic visit it would prove to be. We went inside and were immediately struck by the Spanish-style beauty of the place. It had intriguing little nooks and crannies dotted here and there, a cool stone interior and a friendly, homely feel all of its own. The vista of natural beauty over the valley and the sea was unlike anything I had previously seen. It was unparalleled and took my breath away. There were two unique, little pagodas on the terrace across the road from the hotel, which had an inviting and romantic charm. The whole place was just magical. We met with the hospitable and very welcoming manager, Brian, had our coffee and left, feeling all the better for our visit.

As Steve and I continued discussing our plans for getting married, it became clear that we could not really afford to go to Hawaii as we hoped. It would also be unlikely that our family and friends would be able to attend there, due to the high cost of visiting, but I did not really mind as I was in love with Gozo. I could think of no better place to hold our special day than in the place we had made our home. We were, however, still stuck on where to have the big day. I googled wedding venues in Gozo and was bombarded with information. We spoke to local people who recommended various places, but none had that extra 'something' for which we were searching. We were starting to feel that we would never find the right place. We had almost forgotten about the magical, little hotel tucked away in Xagħra, just waiting for us to make the decision.

One day, exhausted with considering all the options, it seemed that we both remembered the hotel at the same time.

"What about that little place we went to in Xagħra that day?" said Steve. "That was really lovely."

"I was just thinking the same thing," I said, excitedly. "It's perfect."

We both realised that the *Cornucopia* had all the right ingredients for our special day and we made the decision to get married there. After making enquiries, we discovered that we could have both the ceremony and the reception at the hotel. All we had to do was provide the correct paperwork, inform the Registry Office about the date, arrange for transportation to get the relevant official to the hotel and that was it. Simple, no?

Hmm, not as simple as I thought. We both had to provide full birth certificates, which I did not even know existed. Those were not your conventional birth certificates, but ones that also showed both your parents details on them. We already had local identity cards, passports and proof of our respective divorces, so we thought were all set. But then we were told that we had to provide proof from someone who had known us for more than three years; that neither of us had been married since our divorces. That was probably the most complicated piece of documentation we had to provide, but still not too difficult. We arranged for Steve's mum in the UK to go to a solicitor and sign the relevant documentation, which she then posted on to us in Gozo. We were all set.

Being a fairly unconventional couple, we did not want to have a traditional, formal wedding in the sense that there would be seating arrangements, speeches and all that jazz. We had both been married before and wanted something different. I could not have been more excited in planning our big day and immediately went into hyper-drive, scouring *Amazon* for wedding accessories. We had friends and family who were teachers, who obviously could not take time off during term time, so we had agreed on the October date when it would be cooler and less expensive for them to travel to Gozo. Meanwhile, I ordered rolls and rolls of white, blue and turquoise organza from good old *Amazon* who delivered everything at a surprisingly reasonable rate. I intended to decorate the hotel with those colours, along with table sparkles, balloons and a host of other goodies. It was so much fun, planning and organising the wedding! I was in heaven.

We went to speak with Brian, the manager of the *Cornucopia,* and explained to him exactly what we wanted on our day. He could not have been more accommodating and agreed to all our requests. However, we had one request yet to make, which we were fairly certain was unique. We wanted our old lurcher, Ollie, to be our best man.

By now, Ollie was 20 years old and had been my faithful friend for 19 of those years. When I met Steve, he had adopted Ollie and loved him too. We both wanted him to be part of our day as we realised that we might not have him with us for much longer. Steve explained that to Brian who, to his eternal credit, never missed a beat. He agreed immediately, which confirmed to us – as if confirmation were needed – that we had chosen the right venue. The outdoor pagoda, which we had seen on our initial visit, was perfect for the ceremony. Brian agreed that we could decorate it as we wished and assured us of his best attention for our day. The menu was sumptuous and to our own requirements. Nothing was too much trouble and even in the planning stages, we felt very special.

We did not know many people in Gozo at the time, but invited those with whom we had become friends. Of course, we also asked some of our friends and family from the UK, and were grateful for those who managed to make the trip over to celebrate the day with us. Steve got a bit carried away with it all and took to inviting people at every opportunity, including at gigs.

"We're getting married soon and you're all invited," he would announce to the whole crowd.

There would be a big cheer and I would have to explain that they were, in fact, *not* all invited as we were not millionaires.

As our big day approached, I was anxiously scanning the skies to see if the weather would hold out for us. October can be really gorgeous in Gozo, but it can also rain a fair bit and as our wedding was at the end of the month, there was always the chance that it would rain on our parade, so to speak. Steve would repeatedly reassure me as best he could.

"So what if it does rain? Nothing can spoil our day," he would say.

Little did we know that what lay ahead was far more devastating than a bit of rain.

The week prior to the wedding, many of our guests started arriving. Most of them were also staying at the *Cornucopia*, so they would be on site for the day. We had Steve's daughter, Sabrina, staying with us, along with his mum, known to one and all simply as Nannan. The festivities continued along with the planning. Everyone was roped in and given a job, even if it only entailed blowing up balloons or wrapping up the tiny table gifts we had got for everyone.

Our dear friend, Manwel, who was a stonemason generously made us a stone tea-light holder for each guest to take home with them – a memento not only of our wedding, but also of a traditional Gozitan craft. I wrapped all the tea-lights in turquoise organza, with a tiny *Thank You* note in each one and secured them with a ribbon. We also had mini packets of *Love Hearts* and heart-shaped chocolates to go in. It was all such good fun. Manwel and his lovely partner and our good friend, Honor, agreed to act as our witnesses – two were required by law. My dear friend, Heather, had agreed to be my matron of honour. We did not go for bridesmaids or pageboys as they were too traditional for our liking. Heather's husband, Greg, a towering eccentric of a man who turned up on the day complete with top hat and all, scripted a brilliantly comical poem that was exactly the kind of thing we loved and wanted.

We had a pre-wedding drinks party on the Wednesday prior to the wedding, when most of our guests arrived. It was a great success, with our large, rowdy group commandeering the lounge of the *Cornucopia* and carousing until the small hours. I did not want the week to end. The day before the wedding, Steve and I booked into the hotel where we would be staying until the day after the wedding. That meant leaving Sabrina and Nannan at our flat, looking after our best man, Ollie. They would join us on the day and stay the night along with ourselves.

I was in a state of high excitement. Our wedding day was so close and I could not wait to be the bride of someone whom I knew truly loved me. I had just about starved myself down to a reasonable weight, to get into that stunning dress. My nails were done, my hair was to be done on the day and everything was in place. We still had to decorate the hotel and the pagoda, which could not be done until the actual day, but I did not need to worry as people volunteered to assist us with that and like everything else, it went according to plan.

The night before the wedding, Steve and I had a wonderful dinner in the hotel with our friends who were staying there, then in great celebratory style, we all went back to our honeymoon suite for a bottle or two of champagne. We spent the evening laughing, swopping stories and generally having a wonderful, happy time. We blew up balloons and Greg worked his artistic magic in drawing caricatures on them for the big day.

Finally, it was midnight: time to say goodnight. As we hugged the last of our friends, Steve and I had a moment to be alone. It was at that precise moment that my mobile phone rang. I smiled, thinking it would be someone ringing to wish us well for the day.

"Hello," I said, still smiling.

"Is Steve there?" asked a serious voice at the other end.

I recognised the voice as that of Steve's half-sister.

"Yes, he's here. What's up?" I asked, slightly anxious at her serious tone.

"Can you just put him on?" she asked, flatly.

My heart skipped a beat. It was obvious that something was wrong. I passed the phone to Steve, whispering to him who it was. As she spoke, he listened and I watched in horror as the colour drained from his face.

"What is it?" I whispered. "What's the matter?"

I felt a cold hand grip me as Steve continued listening and then started replying in short, hard sentences. He got off the phone and I stared at him in dreadful anticipation.

"My sister's died," Steve declared, finally.

And he broke down.

CHAPTER 20

The Wedding

Steve was told that his sister, Jean, had died suddenly and unexpectedly only hours before in the UK. She had been with their aunt when it happened. Jean had not been unwell and her death was a total, devastating shock to the entire family. Needless to say, Steve was overwhelmed with grief and shock. I immediately went to Heather's and Greg's door for support, which they offered unconditionally. With Greg's help, Steve managed to go down to *Reception,* to inform the hotel staff about the terrible circumstances which had just been relayed. He also told them that we needed another room. Steve and I then had the unenviable task of going back to our flat, to break the sickening news to his mum and daughter. How do you even begin to tell someone that their daughter has just passed away?

Both of us cried the whole way there and with great trepidation, made our way into the flat where, of course, poor Nannan was asleep. When we told her, Nannan's grief eclipsed everything. It was total, raw, unashamed pain and simply one of the saddest things I have ever been part of. I shall not dwell on it here. We took Nannan and Sabrina, and, of course, old Ollie back with us to the hotel. I spent the night with Nannan and kept the hotel staff busy with requests for trays of tea. They were marvellous: even at 3.00am and 4am, tea kept arriving. Steve had Sabrina in a twin room with him and tried, as best as he could, to reassure her in what was a nightmare situation. Then the morning of our wedding day dawned and Steve asked me the question which had been left unasked all night.

"Do we cancel the wedding?"

We agonised about it. Would it seem insensitive to go ahead with our wedding in such tragic circumstances? What would people think if we carried on? Would it seem like we did not care? Finally, Steve spoke.

"Jean would not have wanted us to cancel it," he said. "She would say, 'Don't be daft. Get on with it.'"

So after much deliberation, we decided to go ahead with the day as planned. To say that it was difficult is an understatement. Despite the fact that it was our wedding day, I felt a tremendous amount of guilt for feeling any happiness, given the circumstances. I was happy, yet at the same time I was crushingly sad for Steve, his mum and the whole family. However, everyone was marvellous. All our guests offered their sympathy and condolences, and understood if one of us needed some time out to shed understandable tears.

Steve was extremely strong. He threw himself into organising all the decorations, giving instructions as to how he wanted the main event hall to be done. Everyone helped not only with that, but also with the pagoda outside where the actual ceremony would take place. It looked stunning, all decked out in turquoise, blue and white; with balloons, sparkles and matching tablecloths.

I was so proud of all my friends and family who supported us so brilliantly. As the bride, I was whisked off to have my hair done and be pampered in general. I had my most trusted and closest friends with me, along with my eldest daughter, Steff. I am eternally grateful to my old school friend, Nick, who produced a much-needed bottle of champagne for us all to share in my dressing room. Hair done, dress on, makeup finished. Finally, I was ready.

Steve's dad had agreed to give me away as my own parents had passed away many years before, but I was now almost overwhelmed with sadness as he prepared to give me away after having just lost his own daughter. As the wedding music began and I got ready to walk up to meet my wonderful groom, Steve's dad held out his arm to me.

"Shall we?" he said, graciously.

I had chosen to walk in to the theme *If You Get Caught Between the Moon and New York City* from the film *Arthur*. As the music started, I felt my knees almost give way, but Steve's dad held my arm.

"Come on, lass," he said.

And off we went. As I walked into the sunshine of that day, I saw the smiling faces of all our friends and family around us. No one truly knew the full extent of the fight that was going on inside me, not to break down and cry. It was a bittersweet moment as I finally got to Steve's side. It was a long, difficult road, but we had arrived. It was our wedding day.

The ceremony went without a hitch. Our ever-faithful lurcher, Ollie, performed his role as ring-bearer and best man with the aplomb and dignity befitting a dog of his advanced years. He was the absolute star of the show and I am not one bit unhappy to report that he unashamedly stole my thunder and received way more fuss than the bride! After the ceremony, we had champagne and canapés outside in the sunshine, before moving inside to have the best possible party we could under the circumstances. The staff at the hotel had, apparently, never seen anything like it. By request, Steve and I sang a few songs and persuaded them to come out of the kitchen and have a dance. Then it was on to the 60's and 70's disco. Everyone danced and sang, and seemed to make an extra effort to have fun.

Jean was most certainly a part of the day, with a special toast to her memory. Steve was right: she would not have wanted it any other way.

Ramla Bay

CHAPTER 21

Bipolar Disorder

We had only been married for a month when we reluctantly agreed that in light of having spent almost all our recently saved money on the wedding, I would have to return to the UK for another short contract of work. This time around, I was more organised with the accommodation and managed to secure a modern, two bedroom flat in a gated community in Leeds, which I shared with my colleague, the lovely, scatter-brained Amanda.

I still made the 3500 miles, round trip commute back to Gozo every two to three weeks. Other workmates commented that they would never complain about their commute to work again, when they learned of my regular trips home. It was on one such trip home that I stood in our flat and looked around with a critical eye.

"We have way too much stuff," I declared to Steve who sat minding his own business.

Before I met him, Steve had been an avid collector. No, let me be honest: he was an all-out hoarder and had collections to rival those in museums. The Elvis memorabilia alone that Steve had would put *Gracelands* to shame. I am not kidding. We had started out displaying just about everything we could. We had flight cases draped with his collection of American flags and covered in collectables. The walls were adorned with tapestries, limited edition pictures and those metal signs you see in bars. He had 17 guitars plus trumpets, violins, accordions, saxophones, harmonicas, keyboards and so on; all on display. Add to that the posters of his singing exploits, newspaper cut-outs and photos of himself with various celebrities. You get the idea.

The walls of the flat looked fabulous, but with the terrible damp in Gozo, Steve's precious collections began to deteriorate. I would take pictures off the wall to dust them, only to find, to my horror, that they were covered in a layer of green mould on the back. We had dehumidifiers on just about 24/7 which helped, but then we would get the electric bill and wonder for how long we would be able to keep it that way. In short, we reached the conclusion that things had to go and Steve set about downsizing. It was no small task. To be honest, we are still at it almost four years later.

Steve agreed that while I was away, he would busy himself with two things. First, he would sort through all his stuff. Second, he would try to write songs again and record them to his own music. That was a major breakthrough for him as Steve suffers from depression. More specifically, he has bipolar disorder which manifests itself in a number of ways. Bipolar disorder is sometimes known as manic depression, for good reason. On a down day, sufferers might be depressed to the point of suicide or just quiet and subdued. On an up day, they could be manic, irrational and spontaneous to the point of being utterly ridiculous.

One thing for which Steve had lost motivation was to start writing and recording, so when he said that he felt up to doing it again, we immediately bought a 24-track studio for the task. The idea was that when he was alone, instead of becoming increasingly depressed, Steve would have a focus and could work and record once again. It was a huge step forward in terms of his mental health. You might ask, why did he not simply go out and spend time with the wonderful friends we had made on the beautiful island of Gozo, avoiding loneliness while I was away? Well, one of the many ways in which the depressive part of bipolar disorder affected Steve was that he tended to isolate himself.

~ ~ ~ ~ ~

Steve is a naturally shy person, which – I know – sounds ridiculous, given his chosen profession as an entertainer, but his stage persona is nothing like the man himself. It is an act, like a clown putting on his mask and makeup. When Steve gets a microphone and hears music, he comes alive and even if he is having a 'down' day, he can get up and entertain like a man on fire.

Steve and I had met when I went to watch him perform, and we had fallen unashamedly head over heels in love with each other. For a while, like others in that enviable position, we had lived in a bubble. We were oblivious to anything else and all our energy went into our new, exciting relationship. Steve was highly attentive, loving, considerate and kind. He was also, unbeknown to me at the time, mentally quite unwell. He was, in short, a ticking time-bomb on countdown to self-destruction.

I was, naturally, oblivious to all that and had no idea that the man with whom I had fallen in love was labouring under such a burden. Steve had told me that he could be moody, but to be honest, I was so in love with the man, he could have said anything.

Steve could have said, "By the way, I'm a serial killer."

I would still have smiled and replied, "That's not going to be a problem."

But when we had originally moved in together, Steve's condition deteriorated. It was as though he finally got to be with me fulltime, then simply shut down with the sheer effort it had taken to get to that point. He refused to do any more shows. He ceased to get out of bed all day, stopped taking a shower and generally turned inward on himself. It was like watching a hedgehog curl up into a tiny ball of self-protection, prickles facing outward.

Communication was painful as the effort of speaking was too much for him. I would go to work at 8.00am and he would still be in bed when I got back at 5.00pm. I took to returning home in my meagre, 35-minute lunch break just to make sure Steve had eaten and taken a drink. By the time I had driven the 10 minutes home, made him a sandwich and drink, and driven back to work again, my lunch break was gone. I am eternally grateful that we had our two wonderful lurchers with us at the time as

Steve had to get out of bed to let them out, but he would always return to his pit of misery.

The boys loved him and as many pets do, they seemed to sense his pain. Ralph, in particular, took to lying on the bed with Steve, nose tucked under his armpit in silent sympathy. Ollie would lie beside him on the floor, ever watchful. Never underestimate the power of a dog's love. Steve is the first to admit that they played a major role in his recovery. What I will also never forget, however, are the spiteful words spoken by people at work who were ignorant of Steve's illness. They nudged each other and whispered:

"We all know why she's nipping home, don't we?"

Add to that the war zone which was inevitable in our divorces, along with the horrendous rumours and downright lies which were being told by our respective ex-partners at the time, it was small wonder that Steve was unwell.

I despaired. I felt totally helpless and had no idea how to get Steve back on his feet. Anyone who has suffered from the debilitating condition known as bipolar disorder or who has tried caring for a loved one who is suffering from it, will understand what I mean. I blamed myself, of course. I was convinced that Steve had regretted his decision to move in with me. *Therefore, it was my fault,* I thought.

Nothing Steve said to the contrary made any difference. I lost count of the hours and hours in which I cried. I missed Steve the man with whom I had fallen in love and wanted him back. His mood affected me and I got to the point where I could not eat. I lived on coffee and nervous energy. My weight dropped. I went from a size 12 to a size 6 in less than three weeks. Colleagues and friends began worrying and told me that I was too thin. However, I was trapped in a vicious circle and did not know how to get out of it or help Steve.

Life is a funny thing. You never really know which direction it might take or how things will turn out. Never in my wildest dreams had I imagined that I would be placed in such a position: helpless, impotent, unable to help the man with whom I had fallen so deeply in love. Inevitably, the situation took its toll on me and I ended up on antidepressants. Never in my life had I been depressed; I felt like an abject failure. It was not meant to be like that. For goodness sake, Steve and I were in love! Totally in love. We knew that we were meant for each other, so how on earth could all that be happening to us?

Steve had days so dark that he would wake up in the mornings and wish to die. He seriously contemplated taking his own life, but to be honest, I simply did not think that he had the energy to pursue it. He had no control over his thoughts. They were a never-ending intrusion on his mind, wearing him down, sending him into the shadows of obscurity and loneliness. His depression was like a snake winding itself around his heart and soul, strangling the life out of him.

While Steve's suffering was terrible and painful, depression – whether as part of bipolar disorder or otherwise – also has a devastating impact on the person who is in the caring role. To watch someone you love struggle to come to terms with their inner conflict and be defeated over and over again is almost too much to bear. It is totally draining to watch as the person is overwhelmed and crushed by something out of their control. I developed a raging resentment and anger towards the illness. I saw it as the enemy in our midst, so I spent a long time researching Steve's condition and began understanding more about it.

When you understand your adversary, you gain more power in overcoming it and attaining victory. I finally reached a place of accepting that Steve could not help how he responded. He had no dominion whatsoever over his mood. He simply could not just "cheer up" and on the rare occasions when we did go out in those days, it would exhaust him and require days of recuperation.

When I had left my ex, most of my 'friends' at the time had deserted me. I do not say this with any hint of self-pity; I am simply stating a fact. However, I had the unswerving support of my eldest daughter and the support of two of my oldest, dearest friends. Without their help, I doubt that I would now be seated here, writing this. I extend my love and thanks to them once again in a heartfelt way. They know who they are.

Everything came to a head on one dismal, January day. Steve had been living with me for a month and had hardly got out of bed in all that time. I was at the end of my wits. One day, I sat on the bed, held his hand and wept.

"Tell me what to do to help you. This cannot go on," I just said.

I had said similar things before, but at that particular time it seemed to hit a nerve. For the first time in many weeks, Steve looked at me clearly.

"If you really want to help me, ring my psychiatrist," he replied.

Upon hearing that statement, my entire world tilted. *Did he say 'psychiatrist'??*

"You have a psychiatrist?" I asked, dumbfounded.

Steve nodded and gave me the name of the psychiatrist. After that, he turned his back on me, rolled over and that was it; the conversation was over. I was on the phone to the hospital within 60 seconds and miraculously, I was put through to the right man. I explained who I was and told the psychiatrist that I was Steve's new partner. The psychiatrist immediately responded:

"Ah, Steve. I wondered how he was doing. He's not been to see me for ages."

Again, I was speechless. Apparently, Steve should have been visiting this doctor on a regular basis. Then the next shock came.

"Is he taking his medication?" the psychiatrist added.

I stood open-mouthed at the other end of the phone.

"What medication?" I managed.

"Ah," the doctor replied, sounding worried, "Steve really needs to take medication to maintain a stable mood. Without it, he will quickly deteriorate."

Suddenly, it all made sense. The psychiatrist explained that Steve suffered from bipolar disorder and that he required meds to keep him sane and functioning. When Steve had told me that he could be moody, it was his way of trying to warn me about his condition. Talk about understating a fact!

I told the doctor that Steve had no medication and he immediately said to go to the hospital and pick up a prescription. I felt elated. There was help and I could go get it immediately! Then the doctor threw me a curve ball.

"And how are *you*?" he asked with an accent on the last word.

That was it; I dissolved. Again, those of you with experience of caring for a mentally ill loved one will understand how a few kind words of enquiry into how you are coping will reduce you to a puddle on the floor. The psychiatrist listened patiently as I poured out a torrent of pain and sadness. He empathised and said that I should have a counsellor just for myself, to support me through all that. I was amazed. Up to that point, I had lived in complete ignorance of bipolar disorder in relation to Steve and here I was, suddenly being offered one-on-one support just for myself. The doctor continued saying that Steve would be allocated a community psychiatric nurse who would immediately begin visits. I put the phone down with a huge weight off my shoulders. *It was going to be okay.*

I got the medication and watched as my beloved man slowly returned back to me, although it was a long, hard road with many bumps and turns along the way. Throughout it all, Steve would say that no matter what, I was not to fret about us: *we were okay*, even if his mood told me otherwise.

He loved me and wanted to be with me. That was hard to accept on days when Steve was not coping with life and he took himself off to bed again. Worse still, he could be seated next to me and not speak for hours or days on end.

I had to restrain myself from constantly asking, "Are you okay? Is it me?"

And so forth. It is the worst thing one can do to a person who is depressed as it only serves to grind them further down. Actually, it is not the worst thing: that would be when people who are rather insensitive tell those who are depressed to pull themselves together. Or worse still, when people tell those who are depressed to be thankful for what they have and draw irrelevant comparisons. Bipolar disorder and its depressive aspect is no respecter of persons. In fact, it is one big, disrespectful sonofabitch; full stop. You can have all the fame and money in the world, and still suffer from it. It has nothing to do with material things. If it did, then we would not witness the steady stream of celebrities dying, miserable and alone in their hotels, from alcohol and drug-related incidents.

After many months of regular medication, Steve – the Steve I had originally known – began to reappear. I tried to make sure that he ate healthy foods, which was easier said than done as he is the fussiest person in the world to feed. He likes all the wrong stuff and when his condition was at its worst, he would eat nothing but packets of crisps. I am eternally grateful that he is teetotal, so that great depressor alcohol was never an issue for him.

There came a day when Steve felt ready to come off the medication. I was understandably nervous and told him so. I could not bear the thought of him reverting back to where he had been after such a long, hard fight. Steve promised that if he felt himself going down, he would go back on medication. Sadly, that was the case; it was too soon. There was still too much going on. While my divorce had been finalised, Steve was in the middle of his and it was acrimonious and bitter. It wore him down again. No, the time was not right. Not yet.

When we made the decision to move to Gozo, Steve was in a much better place. He had made a firm, clear decision not to take any more medication and although there were one or two blips, he has been pretty stable ever since. I am not saying he is 'normal,' though. Steve will never be normal; he is too eccentric for that.

Steve tended to be more open about his condition and willingly told people that without me, he would not be there. I only say this here to make the point that people with bipolar disorder and its depressive component *need* someone who is patient and understanding, giving them unconditional love in bucket-loads. There were times when I doubted my own sanity and at times felt like giving up, but I did not. Bipolar disorder is a completely selfish condition, but the way it makes your loved one behave is not personal. I knew that Steve was in there, somewhere, and I was damned if I was ever going to give up on him. He had loved me like I had never been loved before and he deserved everything I could give him in return. Everything!

~ ~ ~ ~ ~

Steve still has his moments. Some days he is pretty quiet and non-communicative, but those days are rare. After nine years together, I know him well enough and understand that on days like those, it is best to give him the space he needs and leave him alone, albeit with a lot of reassuring hugs. If you ask him, Steve will tell you that the sunshine and peace of Gozo played a large part in his long road to recovery.

While I was away working in the UK again, Steve suffered a major setback. He had spent six months putting all his effort into writing and recording, and had saved all that work on his new 24-track studio. One day, he was in his music room recording more work when disaster struck: a power cut occurred. His work was lost, all six months of it – a heart-breaking blow. It had taken Steve so long to get back to the point where he felt like writing again and it had all been wiped out in one miserable loss of power.

Despite that horrendous setback, Steve managed to stay strong. He lost the will to write and record for some time after that as the loss was so final. Steve does not have a good memory, so he was unable to recapture all of what he had done. It took him some time, but he gradually returned to writing and recording again – with a back-up power source steadily at hand, so that such an untoward occurrence would never happen again.

Why am I telling you all this? I guess I am hoping that it will give some encouragement to others out there who may be going through the same thing. Mental illness is still a taboo subject in our society at large. There is still a stigma attached to it, to some degree. I used to tell Steve that if he had his leg in plaster, people would be under no illusion that he was unwell, but mental illness is unseen and can be easily misunderstood.

Steve still finds social situations difficult, especially in large groups. Our closest friends know this and are brilliantly understanding and accepting. There have been many occasions when we have been invited to social functions.

"We'd love for you to come, but understand if Steve can't make it," they say.

Invitations phrased that way mean the world to us. For people who do not appreciate the struggle that Steve experiences in socialising, they might feel he is being antisocial – or worse, a *prima donna*. But the good friends we made in Gozo were a steady part of the infrastructure of building blocks which helped Steve to heal and be well. One particularly sensitive, close friend, who had not been told about Steve's condition, regarded him intently one day.

"So you're here to rest, eh?" he said.

Our friend was right. Moving to Gozo was part of the restorative process. Steve has come a long way from his bed in Derbyshire. I am sure any of you who know him will agree with me when I say:

"He's worth it."

CHAPTER 22

Deciding what to eat in the hot summer could be problematic in Gozo. The heat sapped up our energy and often left us with little or no appetite. Steve did not eat salads, making the task all the more difficult. One day, I was alternating between standing, staring into the cupboards, then moving to the fridge to do more staring, then back to the cupboards as I searched for inspiration.

"Do you want to try some potato cakes for tea?" I called to Steve as he sat watching television.

Well, I say he sat watching television. He was more accurately doing that thing most men do in flipping through all the channels – and I mean *all* – while complaining loudly.

"What a load of rubbish! There's nothing on again. Why do we have all these channels when there's nothing on? It's ridiculous. How much do we pay for this? LOOK! That was on last night. Oh, no! Not *Magnificent Seven* again!"

You get my drift, right? I must admit, though, that Steve was right. If I had to endure one more 'survival' programme from Bear Grylls or others of his ilk, I think I would have . . . . . Well, I would have jumped off a mountain. Trouble is, no doubt I would have landed in a hostile jungle environment devoid of food and water, and overrun with poisonous snakes and scorpions, and I would not have known how to survive as I never paid attention. Oh, and just so we are clear: your name is *not* Bear! No one, possibly apart from a Native American, is called Bear. Even then, it would be preceded by the word "Running" or "Sneaking up behind you and about to eat you," or something like that. Anyway, back to the potato cakes.

No, hang on before the potato cakes! What about those ridiculous, backwoods-type programmes on the Discovery Channel about swamp men or alligator-wrestling men, or men who just blow things up because they are inbred men? I mean, come on! It is like watching *Deliverance*, but without the really disturbing bits and definitely without the benefit of the banjo scene. What entertainment is there in watching grown men, none of whom are wearing any kind of garment on their upper bodies, blow stuff up?

"Hey, Earl. Watch me," says the cross-eyed, toothless, half naked one who is wearing a gold necklace heavy enough to drown him, if he were to fall into the creek. "I'm gonna fire my 12-bore through that caravan Ma used to live in."

BOOM! There he goes, making a hole in Ma's old caravan. How — seriously, *how* – is that supposed to be entertaining? Sorry, I need to stop now or I am going to have a nosebleed. Back to the potato cakes.

As I already explained, deciding in our house what is for tea is akin to the preparations for signing the Treaty of Versailles or maybe raising the Titanic. Steve's bipolar disorder can affect his decision-making and memory, so to avoid having no tea at all, I try planning ahead with negotiations beginning at around 10.00am each day, hence the cupboard/fridge staring. Bear in mind, not only can Steve *not* make a decision without a minimum of 12 hours advance warning of the subject matter. He is also hideously fussy to feed.

Steve does not like pasta and he does not like spicy food. He does not eat brown bread; only white. Oh, no; wait! He *does* eat brown bread, but it cannot have any bits in it, so granary is right off the menu. Steve will not eat fish unless it is boneless, skinless and, basically, fishless. Chicken is okay as long as it is from a chicken that did not possess any body fat and was held together with something other than skin. Steve does not like red meat and, oh, forget vegetables and salads unless it is a carrot. He is not keen on rice unless it is the egg-fried variety, preferably accompanied by sweet and sour chicken — boneless, skinless, fatless.

Steve is also suspicious of anything new and if presented with something he has never had before, he will revert to Neanderthal man mode. He will hold it up at arm's length, smelling it and frowning at it for a *looong* time. Then he will drum up courage and venture a taste, closing his eyes tightly shut while he does so. He will 'taste' seven molecules, then say:

"Hmm, it's alright, I suppose. But don't give me any."

Or words to that effect. Finally, he never wants a lot. All tea decisions generally end with the following words:

"...but I don't want loads."

So back to what is known in our house as *The Tea Question*. It generally goes something like this:

Me: "What do you think you might like for tea later?"

Steve: "Dunno. What we got?"

Me: "Well, we could have something simple like beans on toast or cheese on toast. Or if you prefer, I'll make something more substantial. A chicken dinner perhaps?" (*Skinless, boneless, fatless*).

Steve (*Silence . . . . . Several minutes of silence. Too many choices there*).

Me: "Steve? Tea?"

Steve remains in silence as he gives the matter more thought. Meanwhile, I go off to clean the entire house while he is thinking, then return two hours later to ask the same question again.

Me: "So have you decided what you might like yet?"

Steve: "So what have we got again?"

Me (*Repeat as above*).

Steve: "I don't know."

Me (*I'm getting to it now*): "Would you like to try potato cakes?"

Steve reacts much like Peter Kaye upon hearing about garlic bread.

"Potato what? Potato cakes? What on earth is a potato cake?"

Me: "My mum used to make them. Its mashed potato mixed with butter, grated cheese and a bit of flour, then flattened out and fried in a sort of cake shape."

Steve: "I've never had them. Will I like them?"

Me: "I think you'd like them. I can put some fried garlic in; you like that."

Steve: "Okay, then; go on. But I don't want too many. Don't make loads."

Off I go to make potato cakes. An hour later, I present Steve with his first ever potato cake – he was, in short, a potato cake virgin. *Here comes Neanderthal man.* Steve holds it up at arm's length and studies it, then he sniffs it and tastes it. His eyes light up. *Success! He likes it!* It is like the man from *Del Monte* saying 'yes' – a 1980's advert for orange juice, for those of you who have no clue what I am talking about. Anyway, Steve munches his way happily through about half a dozen potato cakes. Then he asks:

"So why have I not had these before?"

I think about it for a while, but before I can answer, he adds:

"Why have you kept these a secret for the seven years we've been together?"

Whaaat? He is actually accusing me of keeping them a secret as if I had deliberately thought *I know, I won't make potato cakes for at least seven years. That'll keep him guessing.* I search for the appropriate answer, but know that none will suffice. Steve loves them and feels cheated to have been deprived of them for so long. Potato cakes are on the menu for many days thereafter. All the while, Steve is shaking his head.

"I can't believe you kept these a secret," he says.

~ ~ ~ ~ ~

The days in Gozo were now gloriously hot. We would get up each morning secure in the knowledge that we could put on our shorts and tee-shirts, and not worry what the weather was going to be like. We had the whole summer ahead of us and could finally enjoy the benefits of living in the Med. We continued singing almost every week and did some outside gigs too, which was great. Passers-by and tourists would stop by and join the fun, even dancing in the streets as the infectious holiday spirit took hold of them.

One downside of summer, however, was the mosquitos. They bite. Oh, how they bite! The bites itch like crazy and in extreme cases can get infected. In my efforts to combat the problem, I had products rivaling *Boots the Chemist*. I had clickers which took the itch out and I had anti-mozzie gel and anti-itch gel. In my opinion, the most effective anti-mozzie gel is the *Jungle* formula one, but it has to be the highest strength, which in Gozo set you back a cool 12 euros. In addition, we had battery operated devices which emitted a high pitched signal, supposedly to ward off the mozzies. Hmmm . . . . . Save your money, they do not work. We had plug-in things which give off some sort of scent, which again were supposed to deter them. Nothing worked – and I mean *nothing*. We ate garlic, marmite, brewer's yeast and everything else, supposedly to put them off; but all in vain.

There are several species of venomous (as opposed to poisonous) spiders, snakes and other creepy crawlies and plants in Malta and Gozo, but nothing that I am aware of will cause serious damage to a human being unless you have an allergy. I once saw a beautiful, two-meter-long, black, whip snake. I was out with Ollie for a walk and saw what I thought was a black ribbon floating across the field. I watched it for a while, marveling at how a piece of ribbon could blow along in such a perfectly symmetrical manner. Once I focused properly, though, I realised that it was a snake. Not only that. I watched it catch a mouse and slither off with it. The snake had probably watched the Bear Grylls episode on *How to Catch Your Supper* and was undoubtedly looking forward to enjoying his mouse, when along came a lunatic woman with camera in hand, shrieking incoherently. I was shouting to Steve on my mobile phone:

"Look out the window, look out the window!"

Another fairly common visitor we had in Gozo were scorpions. We found them in the yard and even had them in the house, which was a bit disconcerting. I once moved a box on the stairs and there was a scorpion right underneath, which rendered me frozen to the spot. The scorpions will, of course, oblige you with a sting if you interfere with them, but they do not really do any serious damage unless, again, you have an allergy. My number one pet hate, however, was the cockroaches. I hated them with a passion and always had a huge bottle of killer spray to hand. Thankfully, I only encountered one in three years. They mainly stayed in the garage, which was fine with me as that was Steve's domain.

One thing we loved doing in the hot weather was to go out on Steve's 600cc *Suzuki Bandit* motorbike. We loved that bike and enjoyed riding it around the island. If you have ever been to Gozo, you already know that safety standards are not quite what they are in the UK. People ride mopeds and motorbikes dressed in no more than a tee-shirt, shorts and flip-flops. We even saw people riding barefoot, the consequences of which do not bear thinking about. We also saw small children – three is the record – squeezed on the front, none of them with crash helmets. Dogs, large and small, also sat up there, ears flying in the breeze. There were men who smoked as they rode and – my favourite – a man enjoying a slice of pizza. We would turn up somewhere in full leathers – boots, jackets, trousers, gloves, full face helmets and so on – only to be met with a polite enquiry:

"Are you not hot?"

"Well, yes. We're hot, but also safe."

"Yes, but is it not too hot?" they would press.

"Err, well; yes. But it's really not safe to ride without full leathers on," we would try to explain.

Our explanations fell on deaf ears. The locals would shake their heads and smile in despair at the mad Brits who went about in 30 degrees of heat with thick clothing on! It was so much cooler in flip-flops.

Steve was a really good biker and took great care of me on the back. When his bike first arrived in Gozo, I had never actually been on it and the first time he took me for a ride, I thought I was going to be sick. I was *so* nervous. Steve despaired of me at first as having spent a lifetime riding horses, I would try to counterbalance every time we went around a corner.

"No, no!" he would exclaim in a cross, muffly voice through his helmet. "Lean INTO the corner. Stop leaning the wrong way, you'll have us over."

It took some getting used to, but once I grasped it, I loved it. Steve's patience on the roads, however, was not what one might call over-developed. It was bad enough in the car where I had to listen to him lecturing all the other road users on how to drive correctly.

"Look at that!" he would invite, gruffly. "No indication, whatsoever. He's clueless."

I would nod in silent agreement.

"Learn to drive!" he would shout, helpfully, as we drove past, tapping his head as he did so, with me sinking down as far as I could in my seat.

The other bone of contention was roundabouts, which reportedly were a fairly new phenomenon in Gozo. Consequently, not everyone seemed totally *au fait* with how to use them. Of course, Steve knew how to use roundabouts and would waste no opportunity sharing his knowledge with others 'less educated' than himself.

"I don't think so, mate," he would say through clenched teeth as we approached, maintaining his right of way at all costs.

And Steve would glare and do more head-tapping when people got it wrong and almost drove into us. The car was one thing, but the bike was another. He was super-vigilant on the bike, especially where I was concerned, which was kind of nice as I like feeling protected.

One day, we were out for a ride. As we approached a junction, a car came dangerously close to the back of the bike. Steve did his turning-around-menacingly-while-glaring-through-his-full-face-helmet face, which was rather wasted on the guy as he did not really get the full effect, what with the full-face thing and all. Anyway, the guy did not back off, but kept trying to squeeze through the gap between the pavement and ourselves, which was clearly way too small. I squealed and whipped my leg out of the way as if I had not done so, he would have hit me. Well, that was it. The guy had managed to force his way through and driven off.

Oh, no you don't, Mr Bad Driver, I thought. *Here comes Steve in hot pursuit.* What followed was a comical, yet really, really scary drive at high speed around Gozo. The driver knew that the game was up and realised fairly quickly that Steve was on the warpath and determined to have him. We chased up hill and down dale, with me hanging on for grim death and praying that we did not hit one of Gozo's famous potholes or I would fly off. After a few miles of giving chase, Steve had definitely scored some points. He had managed to do quite a lot of fist shaking and shouting, and almost managed to pull up in front of the driver at one point, only to be thwarted by the appearance of a small child. I eventually resorted to knocking loudly on the back of Steve's crash helmet and shouting at the top of my muffled voice:

"Stop it. Stop it now!"

But to no avail. The red mist had come down and I knew that Steve would not stop until there had been a satisfying conclusion, which resulted in:

1. Waylaying the man and dragging him bodily out of his vehicle;
2. Berating the man and possibly hitting him fairly hard; and
3. Abject apologies from self-same man;

As it turned out, none of the above happened. Steve eventually caught the driver at the roundabout near the bottom of Gozo, but given that no one knew how to use the roundabout – apart from Steve, of course – there was a lot of confusion. To his credit, Steve managed to drive alongside the car window and gained some satisfaction from banging on it and shouting *a lot*. The driver retaliated by winding down his window and yelling back in Italian. I sat on the back of the bike wondering how we had ever got into that mess as the man hurled one last insult and made good his escape in the roundabout confusion.

Ollie with his blue shoes

CHAPTER 23

The Blue Shoes

As you know, when Steve and I moved to Gozo, Ollie the lurcher also came along. He was 19 years old at the time of our move so it was a risk, but he coped brilliantly with the whole journey and settled into his new home without fuss or ceremony. We were living in a large, first floor flat in Għajnsielem, having moved from the third floor apartment in Marsalforn. However, Ollie did not care where he lived as long as he had his home comforts, which equated to:

1. A comfy bed;
2. Plenty of food;
3. Many treats;
4. Chinese food, hot dogs and tomato soup.

Yes, tomato soup – go figure. That is what he liked and regularly, thank you very much. Like most lurchers, Ollie was a shameless thief who would steal food from right under your nose. He had what lurcher owners tend to refer to as 'magnet mouth.' It is the curse of all lurchers. What can they do? It cannot be helped if food gravitates to their mouths and as it does so, their mouths open as if by magic and *Hey, presto:* food gone.

I digress as I recall an incident with our other lurcher, Ralph, who was a force to be reckoned with at almost six feet tall on his back legs. One night, Steve and I had been providing singing entertainment for not one, but two venues, which was a bit tricky but not impossible. One event was a wedding where Steve was singing and the other was a wedding anniversary where both of us were singing. Here is how it worked.

Steve set us up in both places, then he began his first spot at the wedding, while I sang at the anniversary. As I took a break, he dashed over (11 miles, I hasten to add) and did his spot at the anniversary. Then it was back to the wedding and so on all night. You get the picture? Well, as you might imagine, there were buffets at both events, but as Steve was dashing 11 miles between venues, he never found time to eat. At the end of a tiring, but successful evening, he met up with me again and we packed to go home. Our hostess invited us to take some food home with us, for which Steve was particularly grateful as he was starving. I piled up a paper plate high with his favourites: egg sandwiches, quiche, sausage rolls, crisps and so on, and chucked a few pickled onions on for good measure.

"Take some more," insisted the hostess. "It'll only waste."

Okay, then. More egg sandwiches went onto the groaning plate full of tasty snacks.

"Do you want this now?" I asked Steve as I saw him eyeing the plate with longing.

Steve wavered for a moment, then decided.

"No. I'll wait till I get home and can sit and enjoy it properly."

Off we went as I clutched Steve's hard-earned supper in the front, so as not to drop any of it. I had put another plate on top, to keep all the contents in and it made an effective box of goodies. We got home and I went to let the boys out. Pleased to see us, the lurchers dashed into the garden, doing their usual wall of death run.

"I think I'll unload the car now, rather than leave it until tomorrow," said Steve, dodging as a streak of lurcher whizzed past his legs on his second circuit around the garden.

"Oh, okay," I called back over the chaos. "I'll just pop your food in the house and come and give you a hand."

You know what is coming, don't you?

I put the food down on the side in the kitchen and went to help Steve. The boys had calmed down and were busy with their nocturnal ablutions. We paid them no mind as they snuffled and sniffed around the garden, hoping to find a hedgehog to annoy or, better still, pick up the scent of a fox. Five minutes and the job was done.

"Right," said Steve, mightily relieved to have finished. "Where's my food? I'm absolutely starving."

I went into the house ahead of Steve and stopped in my tracks. The sight that met me was one of desolation. I knew it could not be Ollie; he was too small to have reached. No. Magnet mouth Ralph had obviously got wind of the plate of treats, sneaked back in like the master burglar he was, stood up on his considerable kangaroo legs and thought, *Wow, free food!* Yep; he had wolfed down the lot. All that was left were two empty paper plates on the floor and a few crumbs – oh, and a spurned pickled onion! Steve followed and almost walked into me.

"Come on," he said, impatiently. "What are you standing there for? Let's get in and eat. Man, I'm hungry!"

I was, however, dumbstruck at the blatant robbery which had taken place and had no idea how to begin explaining that Steve's long-awaited supper was now inside the dog. I simply stepped aside. Steve stood there for many moments taking in the scene. He picked up a paper plate and the pickle rolled onto the floor. At that moment, Ralph entered, saw the pickle and, to add insult to injury, decided that he would eat it after all. Then he sauntered over to his bed and lay down. Steve adopted the look of a child on Christmas morning who wakes up only to find that Father Christmas has not visited his house. I nodded in silent sympathy.

"He ate your food," I said, stating the obvious.

Steve turned the plate over in the vain hope that there might be a sandwich stuck to the bottom, but it was not to be. He went over to Ralph who was lying in bed, grinning from ear to ear.

"You no-good, thieving article! You stole my supper! Egg sandwiches and all, my favourite!" Steve told him, very slowly and deliberately.

Ralph realised that the game was up; he was busted. The lurcher adopted that ingratiating look of apology which said:

"Do you know what? I'm most awfully sorry, I can't imagine what came over me, but – you know – there it was. And what with me having these long legs and all, it seemed too good an opportunity to miss. Sorry."

Then Ralph rolled onto his back and exposed his tummy in abject submission, wagging furiously as he grovelled his continuing acknowledgement of the heist.

Now, Steve absolutely adored those boys and they loved him back. They were my dogs before had we met, but had quickly become also his boys. Both of them were carrying a few too many pounds as Steve was a devil for sharing everything with them. *Oh, boy!* They loved that. Me? I had never allowed them to beg at the table or given them many titbits between meals. But Steve? Oh, he would share everything with them, no matter how small a morsel. However, on this particular occasion of the heist, his patience had been sorely tested.

"Can you make me some toast?" he said, flatly.

I did so.

"Thank you," came the small reply.

Steve then took his plate and very deliberately sat down on the floor in front of Ralph, surveyed him in total silence, then proceeded to eat every last mouthful without sharing so much as a crumb.

"Mine!" he exclaimed with possessiveness as Ralph leaned in, hoping that his magnet mouth might manage to draw in some toast.

"Mine!" repeated Steve, triumphantly, as he finished the last bite and stood up. "It wasn't the same as an egg sandwich," he said, sadly, "but at least that greedy lurcher didn't manage to get any."

Steve and Ralph were even . . . . . until the next time. Ah, well. Back to Ollie.

Ollie had his own routine in Gozo. He would wake up at around 8.00am and we would hear the *Tip-tap, Tip-tap* of his claws on the tiled floor as he made his way into our bedroom, to let us know that he was awake and needed to go out. Well, it was more of a *Tip-tap, Thud; Tip-tap, Thud, Thud;* as he negotiated the tiles and the rugs in between. Ollie would stand staring at us until we realised that he was there and responded. If we remained asleep, he would wander around the room, emphasising the *Tip-tap* bits and avoiding the rugs, to wake us. Once he had our attention, I would get up and out we would go.

Note here that I said that *I* would get up. Hmm, not Steve; no. At such times, Ollie was very much my dog. The lurcher loved his walks and despite his advancing years, was able to go for miles. He would totter up and down the roads of the village, sniffing and poking around as he went.

On one occasion, Ollie stuck his nose into an anthill and spent the rest of the day sneezing and shaking his head. That same night, we woke to hear him violently shaking his head over and over again. Concerned, we got up and found him with very swollen ears. *What on earth??* Off we went to the vet's in the morning and it transpired that he had been bitten on both ears by the ants. The violent head-shaking had caused huge haematomas in each ear. *Oh, Ollie!* Thankfully, he soon recovered and was back to his old, mischievous self.

~ ~ ~ ~ ~

Soon the dismal memories of the cold, wet winter were behind us. The days grew longer and the sun became a reliable, daily visitor. It was bliss. We explored the island properly and one of our favourite haunts was the unbelievably gorgeous, tiny bay of Mġarr ix-Xini, which was in walking distance of our flat. It was almost impossible to find this bay unless you knew the way, but we discovered that we could scramble down and explore it at our leisure. Mind you, the trek back was not so easy. It would take us ages to labour back up the steep hill.

We also loved to walk down to the harbour where we would sit in one of the many waterside cafés, watching the boats coming and going. The Gozo ferry would bring tourists over in their hundreds. Many of them would walk past us and we would chat to them, pleased at being able to advise them of the nicest places to visit. The tourists would enviously tell us how lucky we were to be living there and we knew they were right. We felt really at home. One thing we particularly loved was when they thought we were just tourists like themselves.

"So when are you two going back?" they would ask.

We would grin and reply, "We're not. We live here."

It never got old. Ollie would sit right beside us in the shade, accepting a fuss from passers-by as his divine right.

As the summer wore on, the flat in which we were living became hotter and hotter. Without air conditioning, it was becoming unbearable for Ollie. We duly went out and bought a portable air-conditioning unit – and our lurcher totally approved. We would often find the dog standing in front of it, panting happily as he cooled off.

One day, Ollie and I set off for our usual walk. It was a scorcher of a day, but I tried to take as shady a route as possible. All of a sudden, Ollie simply keeled over onto his side. I was horrified.

"Ollie, Ollie!" I shouted. "Get up, mate. Oh, please get up!"

Ollie stayed put, panting in the heat. I was about to ring Steve up to help me when I realised that Ollie was sticking out his legs and feet. Suddenly, I realised the problem. The pavement was too hot for him, so he had done the obvious thing by lying down and sticking his feet out to avoid them burning. I felt terrible. *The poor, old boy!* His feet must have been on fire and I had not realized it. *Right. Okay, here we go.* I got Ollie back onto his feet and managed to make it home by deliberately walking on shady ground. When we got in, I told Steve what happened and we stood the dog in a bath of shallow water to cool off.

We then spent hours trying to work out how to alleviate the problem for Ollie as the summer was nowhere near over. Eventually, after some internet searching, we found the solution. There was a company that made special shoes for dogs! Yes, Ollie could have his own special, thick rubber shoes. The shoes would kill two birds with one stone as Ollie had problems slipping on the marble tiles which led up to the flat, his claws lacking the grip he needed to negotiate them. We had already bought him a harness, which he wore instead of a lead. It had proved invaluable as we managed to 'catch' him several times when the lurcher lost his footing, preventing him from falling. The shoes would provide him with much needed, added grip. After all, an old man like Ollie needed all the support he could get, to keep him safe and sound. I could not wait for the shoes to arrive, which they did in less than a week.

"Ollie, look," I said, holding up the shoes for the dog to see.

Ollie looked underwhelmed as he sniffed at his new footwear. Getting them on was a feat in itself. It took two of us: one to hold his leg up and one to put the shoe on. Finally, we got on all four shoes, then howled with laughter as Ollie set off walking. Unfamiliar with the feel of the shoes, the dog brought his legs up in the air in a massively exaggerated gait as he tried ridding himself of the unwanted accessories. Ollie staggered around, shaking and waving his legs. He reminded me of a horse in travel boots as they do the same thing. The dog eventually got the hang of it, however, so off we went.

Once outside, Ollie seemed to realise that although they were strange, the shoes were helping him. He no longer burnt his feet and returning back up the steps was a breeze. He could now race up safely with no danger of slipping and falling. The shoes also made us many new friends as people would stop and stare in amazement at the dog in blue shoes.

"Why is your dog wearing shoes?" they would inevitably ask.

A conversation would ensue, with people walking away smiling to themselves at the end. Ollie became quite the local celebrity and whenever we went out without him, people would tell us:

"I saw you with your dog, wearing his blue shoes," laughing at the memory of it.

The shoes had done their job; no more hot pavements for Ollie. They, quite literally, saved his sole.

CHAPTER 24

Dog Deaf

It was 6.30am. Steve and I were asleep when we were suddenly and rudely awakened from that peaceful slumber by the all-too-familiar sounds of The Dogs. I use the word collectively as that is exactly how it sounded: like A Pack of Them, A Starlight Barking, A Noyance, A Nuisance. *Woof, Woof, Woof, Woof, Woof, Woof; Yap, Yap, Yap, Yap, Yap, Yap, Yap. Woof, Woof, Woof, Woof, Woof, Woof; Yap, Yap, Yap, Yap, Yap, Yap; Woof, Woof, Woof, Woof, Woof* – and on and on and on. You get the picture, right?

I know dogs bark. They all do, unless it is one of those weird, barkless breeds that I personally feel should have been imported to Gozo as the only possible breed allowable. The barking was incessant, unrelenting, interminable, constant, unceasing, monotonous, at all times of the day and the night. In how many ways can I say this? It drove us mad and I know others who experienced the same problem. Why was that?

I have yet to work out just how dog owners could be so inconsiderate towards their neighbours. Why did they feel it was okay to subject us all to their animal's bone-wearying racket? Barking dogs were a major factor in us leaving our most recent house. It was so exhaustingly intrusive. It woke us up in the morning and disturbed the peace of a lovely, quiet, sunny afternoon. Night times could also be worse. We would lie in bed listening to the barking, hour after tedious hour. My knuckles would turn white as I clenched my fists into a ball of frustration, my fingernails digging into the palms of my hands as I fought the urge to get up, open the window and scream into the night for the barking to stop. Our record for a dog barking non-stop during the night was five hours!

Sometimes, in periods of eye-popping exasperation, it would become too much for us and I would leap into action, fling open the window and yell into the darkness:

"WILL YOU SHUT UP?!"

But it was never of any value. It only served to take the barking frenzy to a whole new level. As the daleks say, resistance is futile. No one seemed to care and no one seemed to take any action. If any of us were to stand in the street in the early hours of the morning, shouting, yelling and generally disturbing the peace, someone would call the police and we would be stopped. Why was it, therefore, that no one seemed to feel the same about the noise pollution created by uncontrolled dogs?

I love dogs and have always had dogs. Naturally, they barked. It is what dogs did and we were grateful to them for protecting us and our territory. However, there was a limit to how long the barking needed to go on. When we moved house, we thought that we had escaped the worst of the dog-barking. But we quickly realised that one of our neighbours was in the habit of simply shoving their yappy, little ankle-biter out onto the back terrace and leaving it there. Naturally, the dog objected for long periods of time, loudly and regularly – and did we not know it! It was not taken out for walks. The poor dog was just shoved outside where it barked and yapped until it was let back in. *Pointless; completely pointless.* There were also plenty of others who followed suit in leaving their dogs on the roof or on the balcony or in the back yard, and there they stayed, yapping and barking until they were let back in, which could be hours later. Some people went off to work and just left the dogs out to bark, annoying the neighbours all day long.

Meanwhile, we heard that in a certain village, none other than the parish priest took action. Yes, the priest; imagine that! Maybe, the barking was also keeping him awake. People received letters – warnings about their over-articulate canines – and were told to keep them quiet. Maybe, there could be public shamings, excommunications or such like; I do not know. But we do know that it was completely selfish, thoughtless and utterly antisocial.

More recently, Steve and I were talking to some friends about the problem and we asked yet again:

"Doesn't anybody care?"

Our good friend, Neil, summed it up nicely in response.

"No, they're all dog deaf," he answered, sardonically.

Maybe, that was it. Maybe, it was just such a part of the fabric of the island that no one really heard it. But until then, until we became dog deaf, we had to rely on good, old-fashioned earplugs.

Xwejni Bay

CHAPTER 25

At the Chemist's

I was home for one of my regular, long weekends and knew that something was wrong.

"I don't feel well," I told Steve.

I knew what the problem was: cystitis. If you have ever had it, you will know the accompanying pain I am talking about. Your lower abdomen becomes an agonising world of pain and it feels as if there is a band of evil hobgoblins taking turns in shoving a burning, red-hot poker . . . . . You get my drift. Let me not be too graphic.

Then, of course, there are the – *ahem* – visits to the toilet. I was visiting roughly every three and a half minutes throughout the night. I would lie there, thinking to myself *It's psychological, it's psychological. You DO NOT need to wee.* But to no avail. Up I would have to get again. Problem was, I was unable to not flush a toilet even if I had only done four drops, so here is how it went:

1. Deep sigh from me as I realised that I had to get up again;
2. Slid out of bed, bumped into footboard at end of bed and said, "Sorry;"
3. Stubbed toe on edge of door, cursed and said, "Sorry;"
4. Banged arm on wardrobe door and said, "Sorry;"
5. Deep sigh from Steve as he realised what kind of night was ahead;
6. Stumbled into toilet, *weed* two drops and flushed;
7. Back to bed, repeating #2 to #4 as I went;
8. Patient, "Are you okay?" from wonderful husband;
9. "Yes, I'm fine; thanks," lie from me;
10. Repeated #1 through #10 all night.

Am I touching a nerve with anyone out there?

By the time morning arrived, both of us were frazzled with the lack of sleep and I was in a lot of pain. I knew that I needed antibiotics. Fortunately in Gozo, it is pretty much akin to having your own personal dealer on speed dial as far as pharmaceuticals are concerned. We could just pop over to the chemist's and buy pretty much everything we needed over the counter. Compare that to your average doctor experience in the UK . . . . . You get it.

My doctor experiences in the UK had generally consisted of a phone call whereby the phone rang for about a day before being answered, usually by a bad-tempered receptionist whose social skills made *Rain Man* look like a game show host. After explaining your symptoms 17 times to the non-medically trained Boudicca, she would begrudgingly tell you that there were *no* appointments that day, despite the fact that you had begun dialling at precisely 7.58am, to *get* an appointment *that* precise day. The receptionist would then suggest that you ring the next day at 8.00am or offer you an appointment three weeks hence.

Thankfully, I was not in the UK. I was in Gozo and knew full well that within 30 minutes, I would have in hand the exact medication that I required, to give me relief from the world of pain that is cystitis. So with confidence, off I went to the chemist. I was met by a lovely pharmacist who shook my hand and introduced herself as Carmen (not her real name, I must add). Yes, she did shake my hand and we were on first name terms from the get-go.

I looked around the busy chemist and asked in hushed tones if she had anything that I could take for cystitis. Her reaction was not too different than if I had just walked in and poked her in the eye. Carmen clapped her palm dramatically to her forehead, rolled her eyes while shaking her head and declared loudly:

"Cystitis! Oh, the pain!!"

Alarmed at that blatant indiscretion, I looked around to see other Gozitan women seated, fanning themselves as they waited for their medication to be ready. They nodded in compassionate agreement and remembered the pain. They sympathised with me silently from across the room. Carmen had the floor now and was not going to miss out on that golden opportunity to work a crowd, even if it was only a few Gozitan grandmothers. She continued with some relish, hand still to forehead:

"Ah, the pain you must suffer! It is bad, no?" she asked, hopefully.

"Yes," I managed. "It's bad."

Carmen then went into practical mode and shrugged.

"It's very common in women, in this hot weather," she said.

Having just been in Leeds for the past two weeks, I grimly thought *It is also common in women who have not seen their husbands in a while!* Carmen said that I needed antibiotics and gave me what I needed. As she did so, the other woman who worked at the chemist's entered. Carmen wasted no time in updating her colleague on the situation at hand. Pointing to me with undisguised delight, she declared without inhibition:

"Cystitis, she has! You know the pain she's in," Carmen added with what I felt was a bit too much enthusiasm.

The other woman was clearly overjoyed to walk into such drama on an otherwise routine day and rolled her eyes in sympathy.

"Cystitis," she mourned. "It's so painful."

By now, I just wanted to run out the door as everyone at the chemist's was joining in offering their sympathies and advice to the unfortunate Englishwoman who suffered so badly. But, no; it was not quite over yet. In an inspired moment, just when I thought my embarrassment had reached its zenith, Carmen loudly asked:

"You want an intimate body wash to go with the tablets?"

I closed my eyes in disbelief.

"Yes, yes. Why not?" I stuttered. "Yes, please. Definitely, an intimate body wash. Why didn't I think of that?"

Carmen handed me the six euros bargain, leaned in and said in a conspiratorial tone:

"Wash over a bowl; it's okay."

I grasped my purchases to my chest and made as if to leave, but Carmen had not yet finished.

"You need a dentist?" she asked. "My brother, he's a good dentist and is close by. I don't say this because he's my brother, but as he's good dentist. Here, I get you his card."

I weakly promised to make an appointment should I ever require dental treatment, then just as I was about to make good my escape, Carmen's daughter arrived. After having similarly been brought up to date on the cystitis drama, which I was now past caring about, she asked me where I lived. Now, that was almost always a mistake in Gozo and so it was here too.

"Aahh," she squawked. "My grandmother, she's in the very same village, behind the church. You know the house?"

"Yes," I lied.

Then I was given a full run down of the grandmother's house: the beauty of it, how she had lived here all her life and had been so lucky to live behind the church. I learned that the grandmother had been one of 14 children, all of whom still lived in Gozo. I was also given detailed descriptions of where they all lived, where their children lived and the state of health of each individual.

Please do not misunderstand me. I love to stand a chat with local people, but not when I am in agonising pain. All I wanted was to go home, take my over-the-counter antibiotics and make full use of the intimate body wash – although not, I hasten to add, over a bowl. Anyway, I finally escaped feeling somewhat battle weary with the full history of Carmen's entire family spinning around my head. I found myself wondering if Uncle Robert had ever managed to get to Australia or if Cousin Michael had made it into university to study medicine. Did Joseph make it to the priesthood or not? I would never know.

Of one thing, I was certain, though. I knew that every woman in Gozo would shake their head in sympathy upon seeing me in the street as they would know . . . . . Oh, they would know!

Ollie on the Virtu ferry from Genova

CHAPTER 26

S teve, Ollie and I had been living in the village of Għajnsielem for two years. I was still commuting to work back and forth to the UK and each time I had to leave, it got increasingly more difficult. Part of the reason for that was due to Ollie's increasing years and deteriorating health. He was now approaching 21 years old: an amazing age for any dog, but for a big dog like Ollie, it was fairly unique.

Ollie had been my best friend since that day many years ago when he had decided for both of us that he would be coming home with me. The lurcher had survived so many traumas in his life and now that precious life of his was winding down. I knew it, Steve knew it and I am absolutely certain that Ollie knew it too. However, despite his advancing years, he was still chipper and enjoyed his life at his new home in Gozo. I am pretty sure he was the only lurcher on the island and had become a bit of a celebrity. He had written to the local SPCA (Society for the Prevention of Cruelty to Animals) and told them all about himself. They had responded accordingly and published his story in their regular magazine. That had, quite honestly, gone to his head as he got even more recognition and hero worship. Ollie had always been a resilient dog who experienced his share of mishaps. There was a day, however, when his luck almost ran out and that was before Steve and I met.

~ ~ ~ ~ ~

Ollie had been about eight years old at the time and my other lurcher, Ralph, was only a baby. I had taken them both for a walk around the stunning Carsington Reservoir in Derbyshire, which was close by to where I lived. It was a hot day in August and as it was Monday, it was very quiet. I drove to a nearby carpark and got the boys out, put their leads on and we were good to go. I checked my phone, but knew there would be no signal in that area due to the deep valley and surrounding hills. *No matter, I won't need a phone*, I thought. How wrong I was! We got onto the tracks in the forest and I let the boys off their leads, safe in the knowledge that it was a totally secure area, with mile after mile of forest tracks where they could run free and not bother anyone or come to any harm.

My intention was to walk the eight-mile circular route and give the boys a really good run. Once off their leads, Ollie and Ralph raced off in joyous abandon. Anyone who owns a lurcher – any dog, really – knows their delight in being allowed to run free. My boys were no exception; off they went. Both were extremely well behaved – apart from where egg sandwiches were concerned – and would come back obediently if called. They did not chase sheep, neither did they behave badly with other dogs they met. In a canine social situation, they would wag in happiness, say hello and move on. No fighting, no fussing. Just two nice dogs out for a walk.

I am a keen bird watcher and Carsington Reservoir provided a feast of birds to spot, including some pretty rare birds of prey such as migratory osprey. With the boys engrossed in exploring new and exciting smells, and running off their energy, I was free to wander and allow my mind to think. It was not a good time for me, personally. I had a deeply unhappy home life and was lonely and sad most of that time. I knew something would have to change soon. The boys were a great distraction and I loved nothing more than to go off with them for whole days, just walking and thinking, glad of their faithful company and unconditional love.

We had gone about two miles into the forest. The peace and quiet were tangible and apart from the birds singing, there was not a sound to be heard. The delicious, outdoor, forest smells drifted up to me: pine needles, moss and earth. I loved them. Through the dappled sunlight in the trees, I saw a flycatcher busy doing what it did best: catching flies in mid-air. I felt relaxed and stopped to watch it, marvelling at its dexterity and speed. Through the trees, I could see the grey squirrels darting around as they began collecting nuts for their winter stores. I smiled and thought *Don't let my boys see you* as I knew a chase would ensue. That always ended with the lurchers hopping around on their back legs, barking and wowing up into the tree in frustration, as they tried working out just *how* those squirrels managed to climb trees. I am pleased to say they never caught one; not once.

All of a sudden, the tranquillity of the environment was shattered and I heard a sound I never want to hear again for as long as I live. It was the sound of an animal in terrible pain: a bone-chilling scream that penetrated right into the depths of my being. I froze as my mind tried to work out what was happening and more importantly, from where the noise was coming. It continued unabated, then got worse – louder – as I was galvanised into action. I knew in my heart of hearts that it was Ollie who was screaming, but had no idea where he was as both Ralph and himself had been running way ahead of me.

"Ollie!" I screamed back. "Ollie, where are you?"

I ran on and on up the hill, that horrific noise urging me on. My heart pounded. I was afraid of what I would find as I knew that whatever it was, it was major. As I got further up the hill, I saw Ralph and my heart flipped as I realised that he, at least, was okay. I was immediately thankful as at only one year old, Ralph had already experienced his fair share of scrapes and accidents. He was a neurotic boy and did not cope well with stress or unfamiliar situations. I could see that he was now anxious and afraid. Ralph was running back and forth into the forest, and I swear that he was looking for me and trying to tell me where to go. I caught up with him and after a quick pat of reassurance, I went into the forest. The sight I was met with was one of the most appalling, distressing things I have ever seen in all my years as a dog owner.

It was Ollie. He was standing with his head down, thrashing back and forth, obviously trying to free himself from something, all the time emitting that high-pitched scream of an animal in dire distress. I ran straight up to him, trying to make sense of what happened. Upon reaching him, I realised what he had done. Ollie had probably been chasing a squirrel or a rabbit and had run headlong into the forest. Unaware of what lay ahead, he had unwittingly run straight into a stick which had been protruding out of the ground. The stick was part of a tree: an offshoot that had grown out at an unusual angle and was just at the right height to run into, for a dog. As Ollie ran, mouth gaping, he had collided with it and the stick had been forced under his tongue, down his throat. It was a complete freak accident, but he was basically impaled. My Ollie was trapped and I knew that he was probably dying.

It was a truly shocking, horrendous sight. To be honest, I almost fainted. However, a complete calm also suddenly came over me and I felt myself emotionally detach from the accident and get a grip. Had I not done so, the grief of Ollie's suffering would have overwhelmed me and I would have given up right there and then. I immediately took off Ollie's collar as his throat was swelling up and I knew that the primary danger for him was choking. Then I wrapped my arms around his body and held on to prevent him from thrashing around. I just held him and held him. *My boy!* Ollie had always been a wily and wise old boy, and he immediately became still; he knew I was there to help. I spoke to him non-stop. I told him that I was going to get him out of that situation and reassured him that he would be okay. I ignored the panic that threatened to disable me and took hold of the stick as gently as I could, snapping it off at ground level. Ollie was no longer trapped by the stick, but I knew that there was no way I could – or more importantly, *should* – remove that stick. I was not a medic, but had enough first aid knowledge to know that all that was between Ollie and his bleeding to death was that stick which was now effectively plugging a massive, gaping wound.

An enormous dilemma arose: I was two miles from anywhere with no phone signal, one seriously injured dog and a panic-stricken second dog. How was I going to get Ollie to a vet? I shouted for help, but only the sound of the birdsong came back. There was no other alternative: I would have to carry him – no easy feat as the stick was causing the dog great pain. Ollie was calm, but in shock. I picked him up, apologising for hurting him. Ralph was bouncing all over the place in a frenzy of upset. He could smell the blood and knew something terrible had happened.

Ignoring Ralph's mini-crisis in the face of a much more pressing emergency, I walked about 300 yards before realising with dismay that there was no way I could carry a large lurcher for two miles. It was simply not possible. Ollie was a dead weight and too heavy, so I put him down as gently as I could, rested for a minute, then picked him up again. Another 300 yards and I had to put him down again, sobbing with the exertion and the knowledge that my beloved boy was probably going to die right in front of my eyes, and that I was practically helpless to prevent it. Ollie's eyes were glazing over and the offending stick protruded, mockingly. Flies were beginning to settle around the blood oozing from his mouth. I brushed them away in anger and picked him up again, determined that I would get him to a vet or die trying.

As I staggered on, a sudden, clear, lucid thought entered my mind. If I could just manage to wrap Ollie around my neck in the way a shepherd might carry a lamb, it would be more manageable. How I did it, I do not know. To this day, I have absolutely no recollection of how I managed to get Ollie into that position, but I did. I also grabbed a highly distressed Ralph and tied him to my waistband with his lead, so that he could not run off into the road when we arrived there. *Right!* We were off and at that point, I was not going to stop walking until we reached the car.

After about a mile, I saw a man walking towards us and almost collapsed with relief. As he approached, I began to babble:

"Oh, God! Please, help me! My dog's had a terrible accident and I don't know if I can carry him much further. Please, would you help me to get him to my car? It's not far. Please?"

To my never-ending disbelief and to his eternal shame, that man looked at me in disgust.

"Hmm, I don't really like dogs. I don't think I can help you," he replied.

Had I not been completely occupied with carrying Ollie and controlling Ralph, I swear I would have punched that man right on his sanctimonious mouth! Instead, I just said:

"Thanks for nothing."

And we kept going. I walked for about another half mile, then the road came into sight. Again, I saw people approaching: a couple out with a small dog. I must have looked a sight coming out of the forest, one badly injured dog around my neck, one leaping like a marlin on a hook at my side and myself with a face masked in fear. I shouted to the couple, again pleading for assistance. The woman immediately bent down to protect her dog.

"It's okay," I called, "they won't hurt him and anyway, I've got them both. Please, help me! Do you have a phone to call the ranger?" I begged.

The woman stood up and looked at Ollie with dawning horror.

"He's had a terrible accident," I explained. "I MUST get him to a vet."

People never cease to amaze me. The next words out of the woman's mouth were:

"Well, you really should have had him on a lead. Then this wouldn't have happened."

Honestly, that is what she said. The woman was really suggesting that in a forest of hundreds of acres, where dozens of people safely let their dogs roam free, Ollie should have been on a lead. I stared at the woman in complete amazement. Sadly, I did not have time to argue or deliver the slap I so badly wanted to administer. Then her husband stepped forward.

"Here, he needs that stick out," he said and went to grab the stick.

The man leapt back as I screamed at him at full volume:

"Don't you dare touch that!"

The woman's husband looked offended.

"Well, really," he replied. "I was only trying to help."

My patience was wearing dangerously thin.

I asked, menacingly, "Do you or do you not have a phone?"

Thankfully, the couple did have one on them. I gave them the phone number of the ranger station and the man went to the road, managed to get a signal and rang up the ranger. I was grateful for their eventual assistance. To say that I was relieved when the land rover pulled up is an understatement. Inside was a young man who was only 17 years of age. He had just passed his driving test and it was his first day on the new job. The young man had imagined that his job would entail doing forestry work, showing tourists around and maybe a bit of tidying up here and there. What I am certain he did not imagine to find was a wild-eyed woman, a half-dead dog and his now hysterical, completely demented sidekick. He did not envisage the wild woman screaming:

"Drive, drive! Get a move on!"

The young man turned white as the fullness of the unfolding drama dawned on him. To his great credit, he rose to the occasion, gunned the land rover into second gear and got us to the vet's in record time. Once we arrived, I realised that I was completely and utterly exhausted. I had managed to carry Ollie for two miles on my own, with Ralph pulling at me all the way. I was spent. I asked the young man if he could possible run into the vet's and tell her what had happened, while I sat with Ollie on my knee. The man did so and within seconds the vet and an assistant came out. Upon seeing Ollie, their faces said it all. Sarah, the vet whom I knew so well, shook her head.

"I'm so sorry, but he's not going to make it," she said.

I sat up, galvanised and angry.

"He most certainly IS going to make it!" I retorted with absolute conviction. "If you think I've carried him all that way for you to give up on him, you're sadly mistaken. Now, I don't care what you have to do or what it costs, but get on with it and do it now!"

Sarah did not need asking twice. Between the assistant and herself, they took Ollie inside. Everyone, without exception, gasped as they saw Ollie with the awful stick still in place and myself covered in blood. Ralph was still *boing*-ing all over the place, his stress heightened by the fact that we were now in his least favourite place: the vet's. Ollie was taken through to surgery as top priority and I was warned by a stone-faced, senior vet that his chances were slim to none. X-rays were done to assess the damage, then out came 'stone-faced' to give me the news. They would need to operate immediately, but the likelihood was that when they removed the stick, Ollie would bleed to death as it was only millimetres away from his carotid artery.

"Just do it," I said. "Just try, please!"

I sat in the waiting room and the enormity of the accident hit me. Every single muscle in my body ached like I had been hit in the back by a freight train. I began shaking like a plague victim and started to cry. No, I did not cry; I sobbed – great, gulping, heaving, gut-wrenching sobs for my best friend who was in there fighting for his life. The thought of losing Ollie was untenable. A woman stepped forward and gave me a tissue. That small kindness provoked a new outburst of tears and as I cried, she sat with me and asked me softly what had happened. As I recounted the story, the woman listened in disbelief.

"You carried him? For two miles? You carried that big dog for two miles?"

Only then did I fully realise the power of adrenaline and fear. Ollie survived as I knew he would. He survived, but only just. He had five operations in all and I am eternally grateful to the *Vets of Starkholmes* in Matlock, Derbyshire for their top-class care of Ollie through that difficult time. However, the accident took its toll on him in more ways than just physical ones.

Ollie became depressed. He would stay on his chair, unmoved by food or anything. I took to feeding him cat food out of my hand as it was all he would accept and that only from my hand. The lurcher would lie on his chair, pick at tiny morsels, then turn his head and refuse to eat any more. After one trip to the vet's where he had been for a check-up on the drainage tubes which had been inserted into his neck, he refused to get out of the car. When I tried encouraging him out, he snapped at me: something he had never done to anyone or anything in his life. Ollie simply did not have the energy or the motivation to get out of the car. I brought him a blanket, covered him up and left him alone. I knew that he was in a world of hurt and I despaired for him. His descent into depression was as real as that of any person and the vet said that it was a form of post-traumatic stress. After six long weeks, I was able to take Ollie for a short walk on his lead. We went up onto the moors, a place he knew and loved. As we walked, the dog's head came up and he sniffed the air. It was a start.

It was three months in all before Ollie became strong and well enough to be allowed off his lead for the first time since the accident. I slipped the clip anxiously and stood back, while Ralph raced around impatiently. The latter had missed his buddy and could not understand why he had not been playing chase for so long. Ollie tottered along for a while, then when he realised that he was free, he set off across the wide-open space of the field. Ollie ran. He ran for the sheer joy of living, his ears flying in the breeze and his beautifully healed mouth lolling open, laughing in delight. Me? I just stood there and laughed with him. I laughed and clapped and jumped up and down, whooping and hollering with tears of absolute joy running down my face. Ollie – my most beloved Ollie – was back despite all odds.

~ ~ ~ ~ ~

Around November 2011, we noticed that Ollie was starting to slow down. At 21 years of age, he was understandably a bit wobbly on his legs, but could still enjoy walks up and down the streets of the village. In

January 2012, however, Ollie became unwell. He lost a great deal of weight and we knew that the inevitable, terrible day was not far off. The most difficult thing was that I still had to go back and forth to the UK, which meant leaving Ollie and Steve, and given Ollie's state of health, I never knew what could happen while I was away.

How can I write about the passing of such a tremendous, faithful friend? I knew the day would inevitably come, but I had buried my head in the sand as it approached, unable to contemplate being without my friend of 20 years. My tatty, scruffy, idiotic, mischievous to the last, old Ollie. Denial was not a strong enough word.

Ollie was with us until February 2012, when he decided that enough was enough. He had battled gamely with his illness for several months. He had done us the honour of being the best man at our wedding and we would always be grateful for that. My worst fears came true as I was in the UK when it happened and that is something with which I have never come to terms. I had said goodbye to Ollie as I always did when I left the flat, but at the back of my mind I knew that it would be our last goodbye. I patted his scruffy old head, knowing that I would never have the chance to do so again, and whispered to him that it was okay if he needed to leave as I understood that he was tired and needed to rest.

"Goodbye, old friend," I whispered to Ollie, tears coursing down my face as I left. "I'll never forget you."

My heart broke. Steve and I hugged each other, and I told him that he knew what he had to do if Ollie deteriorated. From the look on Steve's face, I knew that his heart too was breaking.

I was at work when the call came. Steve explained, through tears, that Ollie had been really ill and needed to go to the vet. We both knew it would be a one-way trip and my grief intensified at the thought of not being there for him at the end, when he had always been there for me. I knew that Ollie could not have been in better hands as Steve adored him, but my feelings of utter helplessness could not be shaken. Our good friend, Manwel, accompanied Steve on that fateful day and both wept unashamedly as Ollie slipped peacefully out of our lives. Thankfully, at work I had an understanding manager who also happened to be a dog owner, so when I entered her office in a flood of tears, to try and explain why working was futile that day, she sent me home. Returning the following week to our flat in Gozo was extremely difficult. To walk in and not see Ollie lying there, pretending to ignore me as he often did, broke my heart all over again.

Ollie never really left us, of course. He was all around us in photographs and never far from our hearts and minds. His precious ashes sat in a decorated box besides those of his brother, Ralph, and we had almost daily reminders as we walked where he used to walk. As is the way of life, we often shed a tear for him, but more often than not we smiled at our memories of him. The silly things Ollie used to do, the lives he touched and the happiness and joy he brought to us all.

Thank you, old friend. You will always be in my heart.

The beautiful sandy beach

CHAPTER 27

I t was March 2013. Steve and I had decided to move house yet again as the flat we had lived in for two years had no outside space. We had grown tired of not having our own terrace or balcony, so we decided to move again. Another reason it had taken us so long to get around to moving was that I was still going to work back and forth to the UK, sometimes for months on end. Once I returned, however, we decided to look for a new home.

Renting a property in Gozo was a fairly straightforward process, similar to that in the UK. There were literally hundreds of available properties. Many of them had stood empty for months, if not years – something worth knowing if you are about to take one on as it may have been neglected for all that time and in need of some attention, to bring it up to an acceptable standard. You can rent through an agent or directly from the owner, but if you rent through the former there is a commission fee to pay. There are many agents on the island, but not all offer the same standard of service.

We approached at least three agents in person and by email, expressing our interest in various properties, but none of them got back to us, leaving us wondering about how anxious they were for our custom. In addition, we discovered that, very often, properties no longer available were left on the websites, undeniably as bait to draw one in. As in the UK, an agent will show you prospective properties, negotiate with the owner on price, then a contract is signed by all parties. All that can be done by the agent or is sometimes conducted in the presence of a notary, which is akin to signing with a solicitor in the UK, although considerably cheaper. The cost is usually shared between the owner and the tenant, and is not usually more than 30 euros at the time of writing. The contract is read in its entirety, in the presence of all parties, before being signed. In our experience, arrangements about the rent were then made between the owner and the tenant, with no further involvement from the agent. The arrangement we personally had was simply to pay the rent in cash on the first of each month. Once our landlady was satisfied that we were taking good care of the flat, it was more convenient for all parties, for us to pay three months at a time.

In our latest move, we had decided to search for a new house without the assistance of an agent, so we put the word out among our friends that we were in the market for a new home. Within days, we had been alerted to several prospective flats and houses, which we made arrangements to view through an intermediary who seemed to be acting as an unofficial agent for several owners. After viewing several, fairly uninspiring flats, we agreed, somewhat reluctantly, to view a farmhouse. Our reticence was financial as we did not feel we could afford the higher rental charges that farmhouses commanded. Our flat at the time was a spacious, light, airy three bedroom, two bathroom property with huge rooms. At only 200 euros a month, it offered excellent value for money. The farmhouse in question was way over double that price, hence our hesitation. Our curiosity got the better of us, though, and we thought *What harm is there in looking? –* our first mistake.

Many years ago, I had experienced a recurring dream in which I lived in a huge house with double French doors overlooking the sea. In the dream, I would descend large stone stairs into the living area, open those huge doors and there was the sea. My close friends knew about the dream as I used to say that one day I would live in a large house overlooking the sea – it was *that* real. When we went to view the farmhouse, there were the huge French doors as we walked through the front door and beyond them the most awe-inspiring view of the sea we had ever seen. The hair stood up on the back of my neck.

"It's the house in my dreams!" I declared in a haze of emotion.

Fatal error. Absolutely fatal, rookie error. I fell for the house simply because of an old dream and failed to allow reason and logic to enter into my thinking. While the house was indeed a lovely property with three bedrooms and three bathrooms, it was old, neglected and in need of a lot of TLC. I failed to see any of that and was completely carried away with the beauty of the view. It also had a swimming pool that seemed terribly glamorous and decadent. Steve's attempts to be the voice of reason fell on deaf ears and suffice it to say that we agreed to take the house on for 12 months.

Our second mistake was to agree to pay the rent for the whole year up front – I caution against this for obvious reasons. When things started to go wrong, which they inevitably did, we had very little bargaining power in that we were not in a position to withhold the rent until things were rectified. But more on that later. The deal was done and we were on the move again, this particular time to Żebbuġ.

Having made the decision to move, we had to tackle the issue of transporting our considerable houseful of stuff over to the new place. Simply looking at all the items we – or rather, Steve – had managed to collect over the years gave me a headache and we agreed that we needed to downsize. Steve had amassed an enviable collection of music equipment over his many years in the trade and reluctantly agreed to get rid of some of it, admitting that even he did not need 10 speakers.

One way of selling items in Gozo is to advertise on the Maltese equivalent of *Ebay*, which is called *Maltapark*. It is a free service and attracts buyers from both Malta and Gozo. However, many people from Malta understandably do not wish to travel to Gozo to view items for sale, so we made it crystal clear in our advertisements that the items were located in Gozo, not Malta. Anyone wishing to see the items would have to travel. We also made it clear that everything was in good condition and that we did not wish to consider any part exchanges. So one day, we started plan A: I made a list of everything that we could advertise on *Maltapark* and on each advert I placed an explanation of where we lived, what condition everything was in and how much we wanted for the items. Accompanying every advert was a colour photograph, so that people would be in no doubt as to what they were buying. Simple, no?

No! Our first, small taste of things to come arrived when I received an enquiry about Steve's saxophone. We had bought that beautiful tenor sax in the UK. It had never been used and was advertised with words to the following effect:

> Stagg *tenor sax in excellent condition. Gold in colour, seen in Gozo. No part exchange, thank you.*

The first enquiry text I received about it was worded thus:

> *Please, what make is the saxophone? Is it in good condition? Please bring to Malta for me to see it.*

I read it and re-read the text, wondering if someone was winding me up. Then I turned to Steve.

"Can you believe it, they've asked what make it is? It says *Stagg* in the advert. Did they not read it properly?"

Steve did not look up from his book.

"Mmmm," was all the reply I got.

I was not finished, though.

"Why are they asking me if it's in good condition? I've said it is, so why ask again? And for goodness sake, I said clearly that they would have to come to Gozo, so why ask me to take it to Malta?" I rambled.

"Just ignore them," came Steve's advice.

"I can't ignore them," I said, "I have to respond."

So I did, explaining everything that I had already said in the advert and stressing that we would *not* be going to Malta, to sell the saxophone. The next text arrived:

> *Please, what colour is it? Here is my address in Malta. You bring it to me and I will buy it.*

I stared incredulously at the text.

"Why are they doing this?" I asked, petulantly. "There's a photograph of it, for God's sake! It's clearly gold in colour, which by the way I also stated in the advert. Why has he sent me his address? What's wrong with this person?"

Steve managed to look up at that point and reiterated what he had already said:

"I told you to ignore them. They're timewasters."

By now I was on a roll of indignation and sent a text back in a fit of sarcastic pique:

> *It is gold in colour as the advert says. Thank you for your address, but as I have already said, I will not be bringing it to Malta.*

The text I received back simply said:

> *Oh, I wanted a silver one.*

It was good for a full five minutes of ranting from me:

"A silver one? A silver one. Can they not see from the photo, it's gold?"

And on and on and on. This process happened all the time. I would get text messages offering us part exchanges when I had said *no* part exchange. We would be offered approximately one third of the value of the items and overall it proved too frustrating to continue advertising. We did manage to sell some items, though, to people who were more than willing to make the trip to Gozo for a good quality guitar or similar. However, they were few and far between, so we resorted to plan B: the car boot sale.

I have always liked buying and selling things, whether on *Ebay* or privately, so it was with some relish that I began preparing things to sell at our planned car boot sale. These kind of sales are regularly held in Gozo from September to June, usually to the tune of two or three a month. The car boot sales are held in Victoria and Marsalforn, and are generally in aid of local charitable causes. It costs 10 euros a pitch and is usually a good day out – that is, if you like getting up at 4.30am to get there by 5.00am.

The problem for Steve and I was that the car boot sales were always on a Sunday and we would usually have been out singing the night before. It was not uncommon for us to get home at 2.00am, unload the car from the gig and load up again with all our car boot stuff, then get two hours sleep before leaving the house at 5.00am to get set up. It was a lot of work for a small return, but it did provide us with a medium of selling our unwanted items. It was also a good time to socialise as many friends would come down or else we would see people whom we would not usually get a chance to talk to, so all in all it was a pleasant way to spend a Sunday. Of course, the remainder of the day was a write-off as we caught up on lost sleep.

Once at the car boot sale, we would engage in the customary haggling that always accompanied such events. For the most part, we did not mind dropping the price a little, but some people always took it too far and would try to get something for nothing. Oftentimes, we discovered that the latter were other stallholders who would beat you down in price, only to turn around and go and sell the item at a higher price in their own stall, if you had been stupid enough to sell it to them in the first place. We learned that the hard way after being stung once or twice, and while we would continue negotiating, we never allowed anyone to take advantage of us again in that manner.

I hereby recall one man who would always approach us with some stealth as if on a secret mission. He would lower his voice to a conspiratorial whisper as he tried to buy for a few cents something priced at perhaps 10 euros. On one occasion, he was trying to buy a brand new watch and offered us a handful of cents.

"Oh, no. I'm sorry," I explained, "but the watch is 10 euros."

The man then spun a long, complex tale of how his wife was in the hospital and would dearly love the watch. If I would only allow him to take it to her, he would return with the 10 euros if she liked it. I briefly wondered if I really looked *that* stupid as I explained that we were unable to do that, but if he wished to pay us the 10 euros and his wife did not like the watch, we would gladly refund his money. The man became quite put out and rude upon hearing that. He accused me of denying his dying wife the chance to have a nice watch. I stuck to my guns and repeated that I could not allow him to take the watch without paying for it and eventually he wandered off to try his luck elsewhere.

The following car boot sale, the man was back, trying the same trick again, but this time with an harmonica he wanted, which – surprise, surprise – he wanted to go and play at the hospital for sick people. He said that he would be paid 10 euros for his services, which he would, of course, return and hand over to us when he had finished his mission of mercy. By that time, I had become less patient.

"Beat it, buddy," was about all he got.

On a more positive note, on another day we were at the car boot sale to sell, among other things, my motorbike trousers. A woman approached us and after some deliberation as to whether or not they would fit her son, she bought them. I mentioned that they had pink piping, but she replied that her son would not be bothered about that. The following week, we saw the woman again while selling at a different car boot sale. Smiling, she approached us and said that the trousers had fit her son well. He liked them.

"Great," I replied. "Glad they worked out for you."

"Oh, but one thing," the woman said. "My son found this in the pocket."

And she produced a ring – one I had bought for Steve. It was an inexpensive dress ring for singing and my husband had worn it when we made our *Mustang Sally* video. After we filmed that, the ring had disappeared and I searched the house for it, for weeks, but in vain. It had been in my trouser pocket all the time and I had never thought to check them before I sold them. I stared open-mouthed.

"Yes," the woman continued, "my son, he said to me: 'Look, mum, here's a ring. I think it's gold, but it does not belong to us.' So it must be yours," she gestured as she handed the ring back to me.

I was so pleased to have it back.

"Yes, it's my husband's ring. Oh, how very kind of you to return it," I called to Steve. "Come here and see what this lady's just given me."

Steve was as overwhelmed as I was, not only to see the ring again, which was of no great value, but at the sheer honesty demonstrated by the woman and her family. We gave her a big hug, shook her son's hand and left the car boot sale that day far richer in spirit than we were in euros.

Even with the sales we had made through *Maltapark* and the car boot sales, we still had a frightening amount of things that required moving to our new house. As we lived on the second floor and Steve was having great trouble at the time with a shoulder injury, which meant that he could not carry many things, we agreed to get a quote from a professional removal firm. Knowing how much that service could cost in the UK, we were apprehensive to say the least as we had so much stuff. I contacted *Gozo Express* and initially said that there would only be a few large flight cases to move. We anticipated that with the help of friends, we could maybe manage the day-to-day items ourselves, but the heavy music equipment would need specialised moving. Not only that, but we knew that the move would require a cherry picker lorry to extend up to the second floor window. The window would also have to be removed and it would need several men to oversee that, for the sake of safety.

Gozo Express came to visit the flat to assess the cost. We were amazed at how little it was going to cost us to move so much stuff and ended up asking them to move the entire contents of the house. They paid a visit to the house to which we were due to move and returned with a quotation for us of under 400 euros – that included Steve's motorbike, which was off the road at the time. We readily agreed to the quotation as we knew that a comparable house move in the UK would have run us into the thousands.

The move went without a hitch and once again we surveyed all the mountains of stuff, which now had to be sorted out anew to fit into our third new house. *Here we go again,* I thought as I picked up the first box. *Here we go again.*

The crystal clear sea of Gozo

CHAPTER 28

It was now mid-December in Gozo. The rains over the past few weeks had been unrelenting and the cause of untold misery. We were living in the new house, lucky enough to be overlooking the Mediterranean – all well and good on a fine day, and in the long, hot summer. We had also been nothing less than smug as we had the added luxury of a swimming pool, but when the wind was blowing in the wrong direction and it was winter, it was quite a different story.

The wind whipped mercilessly off the brooding, steel blue sea, generously bringing with it copious amounts of sand from the beach below. That, in turn, found a home at the bottom of our swimming pool, which at minimum led Steve to sigh heavily and hoover the pool out, or at maximum resulted in a diatribe of rage when the sand had been blown over for several days running. All that was followed by many questions as to why we had to live in such a stupid location. There were also veritable tsunamis of water that flooded in under the doors, to form only slightly less impressive versions of the Great Lakes – and let us not forget the cascades of rain that found their way inside through the gaping cracks in the windows. You get the picture. When it was wet, it was wet; inside *and* outside. It soaked the rugs, the curtains and everything else that got in the way, resulting in my springing into action like a demented King Canute, mop and bucket in hand, frantically trying to hold back the tides. It also stimulated Steve into enlightening me on the faults and failings of the Gozitan design of doors and windows in our particular house.

"Trouble is," Steve began, "there's no weatherboard on the doors."

"What's a weatherboard?" I asked as I mopped, sweaty and cross.

"It's an angled strip of wood with a groove in it, which stops the rain from getting in. This place has none. That's why it rains in," Steve explained, patiently. "On top of that, all the doors are fitted on the inside of the steps, rather than on the outside," he continued.

"Well, can't you put a weatherboard on?" I queried, continuing to squeeze the mini-lake into my bucket.

"Of course, I could," Steve replied, offended that I even had to ask if he was capable of such a mundane task.

"Well, then; please do," I invited, "as I'm heartily sick of all this mopping every time it rains."

I knew that having been set a challenge, there would follow many days in the man cave of his garage, while Steve came up with the solution.

"Hmm, let me give it some thought," he mused, his mind already on the job.

I must digress here to say that, in my humble opinion, having a swimming pool is seriously overrated. When we moved into the farmhouse, we – or more accurately, I – had been overwhelmed by the location and stunning views. I had watched enough American *Reality TV* shows to know that such views were what was known in the trade as 'the million dollar view.' You know the shows I mean; right? Those where people have a budget of around 75 million dollars lying around for the right property and a toothy, over-enthusiastic, underfed, Barbie doll of a presenter shows them around, with the families, all referred to by Barbie as, "You guys," looking around the properties and almost fainting at them in delight. The superlatives would become increasingly more extravagant as each room is shown. There is an unbelievable overuse of, "Wow," and a conspicuous amount of, "Oh, My God"-ding. Once we actually started counting how many times the families said, "Wow," in such a show, but lost it as we could not agree whether a collective family wow counted as one or whether we had to differentiate between parental wows and children wows.

Anyway, annoyance aside, Steve and I were inexplicably drawn to those programmes. We tended to sit in judgement, saying things like:

"Well, I don't like it. Look at that kitchen, it's rubbish and the bath's too small."

Or, "A million bucks for THAT? It's not even got a decent garden and look how close the neighbours are."

And so forth. We were also known to question the age of said clients, along with demanding to know how they came by their fortunes.

"Well, he looks about 15. How come he can afford a one million dollar property, eh? This is a total set up. It's not real, you know."

Yet we continued to watch, fascinated. Anyway, I knew that the views we had in the farmhouse in Gozo easily rivalled any that we had seen on television. I also had a sneaking suspicion that I did say, "Wow," when I saw the view for the first time. But no matter. I was ill-prepared for being the caretaker of a pool. The use of the word "I" here is, of course, foolish. To think that, even for one moment, I would be the caretaker of the pool is as likely as my being able to make a weatherboard. Everyone knew that such a hard job would naturally fall to Steve.

Having a pool is okay when it is doing what it should be doing: being quiet and not demanding any attention. A pool, however, is a high maintenance, highly stressful and extremely expensive accessory. When we took on the farmhouse, the instructions we had received from the owner were, to say the least, economical.

"See this basket here?" he said, waving his arm in the general direction of the pool.

We saw the basket. It was in its own little hidey-hole at the end of the pool, with water lapping into it.

"Yes," we chorused.

"Well, put two chlorine tablets in there every two weeks. It's all that's required."

We looked at each other and shrugged. That did not sound difficult at all.

"Is that all we have to do?" queried Steve, suspicious. "It doesn't sound like much."

The owner took on a pained expression.

"As I have just told you," he repeated, "that's all that's required. Just two tablets in the basket."

"Okay," said Steve, unconvinced.

The following week, we had to return to the UK so we asked our very good friends, Manwel and Honor, whether they would mind awfully if they had to pop by and drop two tablets in the basket. It was all that was required, we assured them; nothing more. Just pop the tablets in and the pool would be fine.

Hmmmm. Within a week, I had received an e-mail from Honor. It read:

I don't know how to tell you this, but your pool's gone green.

There then followed a comedy of errors as our poor friends gamely struggled, in our absence, to get their head around how to really maintain a pool. It was, of course, highly complex, expensive and consisted of considerably more than two tablets dropped into the basket. There were visits from local experts who diagnosed the problem and gave advice on how to rectify it. There were purchases of tubs of chlorine at 100 euros a shot. There were water testing kits, special gel tablets that did something else also essential. And to top it all, a water bowser had to be ordered to visit, to fill the wells.

"Wells?!" I said to Steve in amazement.

I had thought there was nothing else which could possibly surprise me.

"We have wells?"

"We must have," Steve replied as mystified as myself.

I am not sure where I must have thought all the water came from to fill the pool, but I sure as fire did not know there were wells underneath it, which needed to be filled regularly by a bowser – and by regularly I mean every two weeks during the summer at a cost of 50 euros each time!

When we got back to Gozo, our lovely friends had managed to deal with the issue of the pool, for which we were eternally grateful. Honor had drawn up a clear, four-page list of instructions, which immediately appealed to my autistic sense of organisation. There were skimmers and sumps, filters; wells to open, wells to close; backwashes, fillings and on and on in an endless mystery almost at par with the Bermuda Triangle.

"Whatever happened to 'Drop two tablets in the basket,'" I hear you ask?

Yeah, right! After all of the above, we were then formally introduced to the pump room for the first time.

"We have a pump room?" I questioned, wide-eyed.

First, we discovered that we had wells; now, a pump room. That room, it turned out, was a filthy, dirty, spider-infested, cobwebby outhouse full of broken tiles.

"I didn't know we had this," I said in wonder, dodging a particularly billowy cobweb that threatened to tangle in my hair.

That was to be avoided at all costs as it would only end in hysteria and tears, with Steve flapping at my hair to get the cobweb out, while reassuring me that there was no spider still living in it.

Anyway, the pump room was to be Steve's new man cave where he could study the myriad of levers and handles. I was not, under any circumstances, allowed to mess with any handles or levers, but was permitted to stand reading the instructions so that he could carry them out. I hasten to add that such activities could only be carried out after I had attacked the room, assisted by Henry the Hoover and a long broom, while wearing a hat. Cobwebs, remember?

"It's a pump room," exclaimed Steve in frustration as he hopped around outside, desperate to get in and pull levers.

"It's Sleeping Beauty's castle," I replied, bashing at the thick, black cobwebs and squealing as the spiders ran for cover, "and I'm the prince with the big, stabby sword," I continued, slashing into every corner and crevice.

"Well, hurry up," urged Steve. "I need to sort this out."

Finally, the pump room was de-cobwebbed and declared fit for purpose.

"So," said Steve with relief as he edged past me to his station. "What's the first thing I need to do?"

I considered Honor's instructions and began reading them out.

"No, no," I said, importantly, as Steve began grabbing at the levers. "Sump OPEN, skimmer CLOSED."

Or, "Set to bypass, close skimmer."

It was like learning a whole new language and on occasion, for no particular reason other than that we lived by the sea, I took to shouting, "Ahoy!" before giving instruction.

"Do you have to shout 'Ahoy?'" said Steve in a fit of pique as he became startled yet again at my nautical exuberance.

"Okay, I'll think of something else," I enthused.

As a huge fan of *NCIS* (the one with Agent Gibbs in it, not that traitorous LA version), I began cleverly incorporating other suitable naval terms into the task.

"HOO – RAH," I exclaimed after a particularly tricky pump room session.

"That's IT!" exclaimed Steve, cross as he banged his head on the lever as he came up. "You're absolutely banned from shouting out naval expressions. I about knocked myself out then," he continued with more than a little menace.

"Sorry!" I offered, but managed to add a hushed, but sulky, "Semper Fi."

Steve stood for long periods of time in the, by now, pristine pump room. As I knew that he would, he got the measure of the pool in no time and was able to thankfully dispense with my assistance. Having the pool was worth it for precisely eight weeks during summer. At that time, it was lovely and warm, and perfect for cooling off in the long, hot, windless days. But that time soon passed and the day came by when I went to have a swim, dipped my toe in and said:

"Brr, no way. That's gone cold."

And just like that, it was over. No more swimming, no more sitting on the edge with our feet dangling in it as we soaked up the sun. Nope. Once that sun changed direction in the shortening days, it no longer warmed the pool. That meant for approximately 10 months of the year, we had to maintain the pool, pamper it, spend money on it and generally pander to its every whim. It repaid us only with those blissful eight weeks – hardly an equitable trade.

When we finally decided to move from that farmhouse and find one that did not leak, rain in and allow gale force 7 winds underneath the door and through the cracks in the windows, we were vehement in our resolve *not* to have another pool. It was far too much trouble and expense. No way were we having a pool ever again! After many months of house hunting and viewings, we finally found our newest house. It was a beautiful, modern, draught-and-cobweb-free place. It did not leak and the owners were helpful and anxious to make it as nice as possible for us.

Oh, and it had a pool.

CHAPTER 29

Squinting into the empty jar, I announced to Steve:

"I'm out of honey."

"Uh, huh," responded Steve, absent-mindedly.

He was focussed on the task at hand: fixing the pipe on the gas cooker, which had been chewed by the mice who were regular, unwelcome visitors to the house.

I like coffee. More to the point, I especially like filter coffee. No, let me be specific: I like *Lavazza,* Italian filter coffee; the one with the gold packaging. With that type of coffee, I like honey. Not sugar or sweetener, but honey – runny honey – and I had run out. No honey meant no coffee, which was bordering on the disastrous because no coffee meant non-functioning.

"I'll pop over to the shop," I decided.

Now, the shop in question shall hereby remain nameless. After all, we did live on the island of Gozo and do not relish being henceforth stoned and banished for what could be construed as criticism, which it most certainly is not. What I am about to make is simply an observation.

The village shop, I can report, is alive and well, and thriving in Gozo. Many residents rely on those kinds of stores and on the grocery vans, which are regular visitors to all the villages; blasting out their horns early in the morning, to announce their arrival and selling an amazing variety of wares. On that particular morning, I could hear a horn blasting for a good 10 seconds, followed by what sounded like a Muezzin calling people to prayer.

"Oh, la, la, la," he trilled at the top of his lungs, which was followed up with an impressive, "Ooooh, yey, yey; la, la, la," and so forth.

I was fascinated as to what the man could be selling, which deserved such a fanfare of announcement. I walked up to the shop, saying my hellos to the local people as I passed them by, sitting on their doorsteps in the warm sun, and counted my blessings. As I rounded the bend, there was the shouty man with his van. I approached as he was in mid-warble, so I waited politely until he had got it all out. The man looked at me, quizzically.

"Morning," I said cheerily. "That's quite a song you've got there."

The man stared at me, unmoved by the flattery. He clearly knew that he had a good song and did not need some Englishwoman passing by to affirm him. I pressed on, undeterred.

"What are you actually selling?" I enquired, politely.

The man opened up the back of his van to display his wares.

"Fish," he announced, proudly. "*Lampuki.* You want some?"

I recoiled at the sight of the neat rows of dead fish staring up at me with their dead fish eyes.

"Ah, no. Goodness; ha, ha! Wow! No thanks. I'm good, really," I babbled. "My husband doesn't really like fish, but it looks lovely."

I had started walking away.

"He doesn't LIKE?" called the man after me, incredulously shaking his head in despair before driving off, no doubt highly offended.

Finally, I reached my destination. The shop, like many of its kind in the villages in Gozo, was basically someone's front room converted into a shop. The entrance was hung with beads. I had to enter sideways as only one small door was actually open and I was hampered by the rucksack on my back, which stuck out catching on things. The inside of the shop was dingy and cool. As my eyes adjusted to the lack of light, I took in my new surroundings. The owners had managed to cram an impressive amount of goods into the small, available space. Consequently, the aisles were extremely close together and I had to traverse them sideways, like some sort of crazed crab. I shuffled down aisle one, marvelling at the stock of dried pasta, which would surely feed the entire island in case of siege.

There was an overwhelming array of goods on sale, piled one on top of the other, making it impossible to actually select much without causing an avalanche of dried goods, tins and sweets. *Never mind, I'm only here for honey,* I reminded myself, which despite my best efforts I could not locate, so I approached the counter and was viewed with some suspicion by the alarmingly old woman who appeared to be in charge. As a conservative estimate, I would put her at around 80 years of age, but she was firmly in control. She was also otherwise engaged in discussions with another lady who was buying her groceries. At that moment, a younger woman appeared, probably in her 50's. I guessed that she was the daughter and, shall we say, a fairly well-fed lady. *All that pasta, no doubt,* I thought. Anyway, I politely enquired if they had any honey. Now, the Gozitan accent is wonderful. It consists of a kind of singsong way of speaking, very pleasing to listen to.

"Huneeee?" she demanded gruffly, the word inflecting up at the end. "You want Gozitan Huneeee?"

A word of explanation here. Gozitan honey is marvellous and often bought by tourists as a memento of their trip to the small island. It is also expensive and way too good to put in coffee.

"Well," I started, "it's only for putting in coffee, so cheaper honey is fine, really."

The woman spoke to her mother in Gozitan, clearly asking if they had any honey and if so, where was it. I imagined that it would be no small task tracking down the honey in that maze of tiny aisles, but the grandmother knew exactly where all her wares were and gave instructions accordingly, looking somewhat irritated at having been interrupted from her discourse. I followed the woman around the shop, crabbing sideways as the rucksack hindered my progress. She came to rest at the far back corner and stood surveying the shelves.

Ah, there it was. I could see the gleaming jar of golden liquid beckoning to me as it nestled among the jars of jam, marmalade and marmite – yes, you can get marmite in Gozo. The woman, meanwhile, just stood there staring.

"There it is," I offered, helpfully leaning forward as far as the space would allow and pointing.

"No," she replied, firmly. "That's jam."

"Ah, yes; there's jam too," I replied. "But look, the honey's right there, next to it."

The woman gave me a withering look.

"No, that's jam," she repeated.

I could not contain myself any longer and shuffled as close as I could under the tricky circumstances, the rucksack and the woman's undeniably ample hips.

"Pardon me," I apologised as I reached for my prize. "Look, here it is," I triumphed.

"It is jam," insisted the woman, looking at me as if I were an idiot.

"No, no! Really, it's honey. Look here, it says *Miele,* which is actually an Italian and French word, but it means honey."

Did I really say that?! I moved on quickly to smooth over the unnecessary Italian and French lesson.

"Anyway, that's great. Thank you," I continued, "I'll just take this."

With one last shake of her head, the woman took the jar to her ancient mother and went back to the living quarters at the rear of the shop. As she went gratefully back about her business, the woman looked over her shoulders and warned me.

"Take it if you want, but it is jam."

Then she was gone. I paid and left, smiling to myself. I got home to find Steve still fixing the gas pipe.

"Did you get your honey?" he asked, not looking up.

"Yes, I got it," I said, holding the jar up for inspection. Steve glanced at it.

"Is that honey?" he enquired. "Looks a bit funny to me."

"Oh, don't you start!" I replied. "Just put the kettle on."

Freya and Steve during a performance

Chapter 30

It was now our fourth year in Gozo, the place I had been drawn to like a moth to a flame. We had first arrived there in 2010 for a week's holiday and I had heard the call of magic as I stood overlooking Xlendi Bay. It had whispered in my ear, courting and winning me like a bride.

We had relocated to Gozo to start a new way of life, away from what we felt was a deteriorating situation in the UK. Although at the time of living in the UK, I had a good job in England and both of us were busy singing every weekend, everything felt like a battle. Life seemed to be one, long argument. If it was not one of the service providers overcharging us or an ex-partner causing trouble, it was something else and we had come to the end of ourselves with it all. Relocating had been a big gamble, but had paid off. Moving overseas is not something you do on a whim and although we had made the decision fairly rapidly, we had already been talking about moving abroad for some time and put a lot into planning, prior to making the move.

The drive over to Gozo through an ice-locked Europe, although stressful, had pretty much gone without a hitch – if you ignore Ollie's toilet trauma on the *Virtu* ferry, that is, which still makes me wince and smile whenever I think about it. We had found somewhere to live without any problem and had found our niche in the Maltese Islands, providing entertainment for many of the local bars, restaurants and hotels. The resultant friendships we made were, without a doubt, the closest we had ever known. Local people and expats alike, we had a very close-knit group of trusted, loyal friends who could be relied on in any emergency.

I recall an incident in 2011 whereby a close neighbour and friend came immediately to my aid when I was in dire straits. Steve had flown back to do some work on one of the houses we owned back in the UK, but was due back on that particular day. I had stayed at home to take care of Ollie and was anticipating Steve's return on the day in question. I was in the shower, getting ready to go and pick him up from the ferry, when the phone rang.

As you probably know, shower or not, we all want to answer the phone – the ladies certainly do, at any rate. I hesitated, knowing how slippery the Italian tiled floors were and made the sensible decision to let the phone ring. After a few seconds, however, my mobile also began ringing and I thought it must be important for someone to ring up both the landline and the mobile. Throwing caution to the wind, I stepped out of the shower and tiptoed as fast as I could down the corridor, being careful to step only on the rugs I had dotted about like hopscotch squares. I was almost there when I realised that I had run out of rugs in the corridor and had to place one wet foot on the tiles, to step to the next rug in the living room.

BANG! Down I went, completely pole-axed. I fell straight over backwards and my head hit the floor like a felled tree. I was totally dazed and badly hurt, and I knew that I was in trouble. I yelled out in pain – which frightened old Ollie who scuttled quickly to the back of the flat, before tentatively coming over to see if I was okay. Naturally, I was not. The pain in my head and neck was excruciating, and I knew that after such a hard knock to the head, I was lucky to be conscious. My first thought was to ring my closest friend, Honor, but knew that it would take her at least 15 minutes to get to me. I was truly afraid that I would pass out. Then I thought about a friend, Mandy, who lived only three blocks down the street and worked from home as a hairdresser. I crawled to my phone, which had long since stopped ringing and managed to dial her number.

"Mandy," I croaked, "I've had a bad fall."

It was all that was required. Within two minutes, Mandy was at my door, having dropped her scissors and apologised to her startled customer that she had to go. She picked me up off the floor and helped me into the bedroom to dress. Then she took a look at my head.

"Have you dyed your hair?" Mandy asked, casually.

I shook my head.

Mandy let out a small, "Oh."

That practically told me that I had a gash to the back of my head – and a sizeable one at that. Mandy promptly called her husband, Graeme, and between the two of them, they got me to the hospital amid half-crazed ravings from me, predicting my imminent death.

"You won't die," said Mandy, calmly.

I suspect that she was working hard to suppress a smile at my ridiculous premonitions of doom. We got to the hospital where only two weeks before, Steve had been an inpatient with a bad chest infection. The orderly who came to the door took one look at me.

"It's the wife of Elvis," he declared.

Even in my sorry state, that made me laugh. Once in the hospital, Mandy took over, organised care for Ollie and placed a call to Honor.

Honor was with me within minutes and sent a message to Steve who, at that precise moment, was flying overhead and about to land. She asked that he ring her upon landing, adding that there was nothing to worry about. Steve, of course, knew different and upon landing, he rang up my phone which I had given to Honor. Upon hearing about the drama, my husband leapt into a taxi and arrived at the hospital in record time. I shall be forever grateful to our friends for responding so quickly to my emergency that day and to all who visited afterwards with gifts of food for Steve – they knew about his inexistent skills in the kitchen – and flowers for me. After many x-rays and a diagnosis of severe concussion, I spent a week in bed, nursing a massive headache and a body full of bruises. But Mandy was right: what happened had not been enough to finish me off.

That was just one of many incidents we went through, where our friends supported and helped us. At the time of writing, we continue enjoying close bonds with many good people in Gozo, for which we are eternally grateful. On a lighter note, we are also extremely thankful for the loyalty of our friends in their unceasing support for our singing in Gozo. We are acutely aware that such loyalty enabled us to remain on the island, living the life we loved. Over the four years we performed in Gozo, they turned up, week in, week out, to hear us sing and cheer us on. They waved aside our apologies of their having to listen to many of the same songs, week after week.

I particularly remember one lovely, Gozitan lady shrugging and saying, "What of it? We wear the same clothes and eat the same food when we come to see you. So what of it?"

The gigs provided us with some of the best laughs we ever had. When Steve sang the Elvis hit *Teddy Bear*, it sounded remarkably like the backing group were singing *Hot Banana* over and over. You listen and tell me if this is not correct: *Baby, let me be (Hot Banana) your loving teddy bear (Hot Banana)* and so on. Steve commented about the above one day and got everyone singing the refrain instead of the real words. He thought no more about it until the next show when he performed the same song. A large group of our friends suddenly leapt to their feet singing *Hot Banana* and brandishing, yes, BANANAS! They had gone to the trouble of organising the thing between themselves, knowing that it would render Steve speechless – and it did. They were forever more known as *Hot Banana's* backing group and to this day can be relied upon for pleasant foolishness.

On another occasion, our friends secretly bought Elvis masks and as Steve made his entrance, he was suddenly faced with a sea of Elvises all singing back at him. When he sang the line from *Teddy Bear* – that is, *Put a chain around my neck* – they did! Someone produced a chain and collared Steve with it, once again bringing the song to a halt as he laughed. In *Return to Sender*, my husband was promptly faced with an avalanche of envelopes, beer mats and papers as people literally threw them at him.

One particularly memorable evening, we had been booked to sing at the one and only hotel on the smallest island of Comino. That meant taking a boat across the short stretch of water, complete with all our equipment. I fretted at the almost inexistent instructions I had been given as to where we should wait and at what time. We stood anxiously at the edge of the harbour, all our equipment stacked up as we waited, scanning the sea for signs of the boat that was to take us and our 30-strong entourage over to the hotel. Eventually, a large fishing boat sailed into view and the crew calmly helped us load everything up as if it were something they did every day of the week. Off we went.

That night, we sang underneath the stars and the sounds of rock and roll carried far over the water. We smiled in delight as the ships moored out in the bay blasted their horns in acknowledgement and people danced on the decks, waving in pleasure at that unexpected open-air show. The journey home was unforgettable. It was August, hot and sultry with a brilliantly clear sky. It was that time of year for shooting stars and we knew that the weather was forecast to be especially good for shooting stars. As we sailed back with our slightly drunken, merry band who were still singing *Hey, Baby*, we watched in awe as the night sky lit up and the bright lights of dying stars rained down around us. It was another magical night in the area of Gozo and we revelled both in it and in the friendships which emanated love and warmth – oh, and the sound of the slightly drunken singing all around.

Billboard of Steve and Freya as entertainers

Chapter 31

As one day I noticed the tell-tale signs, I said to Steve: "Duh! We've got mice now."

"Might as well have," replied Steve with a sigh.

Off we went to the DIY store once again. Now, I cannot bear to kill anything, let alone with considerable relish, apart from wasps. I have never forgiven them for the two unprovoked stings they gave me when I was still a child. Other than that, I do not kill anything, so we chose humane traps for our visiting rodents.

"What do you intend to do with them, when you catch them?" enquired Steve, eying the plastic contraptions with wariness.

"I don't intend to do anything," I said in horror. "That will, most definitely, be your department. Look at it as a kind of hunter gatherer thing."

I smiled as I paid the bill. Back at the house, I baited the traps and did not have to wait long. Attracted by the irresistible smell of peanut butter, the mice had walked straight in and became instant POWs. The decision was taken to liberate the mice over the end of the terrace. I accepted that there was a drop of around 25 feet, but it was a soft landing and with the aid of my trusty, ship-watching binoculars, I observed the mice on their one-way trip and sighed in relief as they scurried off into the grass below. I suspect, however, that word soon got around that the house on the hill served great peanut butter and if you could stomach the drop that followed, it was worth the trip. As a consequence, we had a never-ending stream of visiting mice.

Another thing that would freak me out at the house was the cockroaches. Thankfully, we did not have them in the house, but they lived in the dark recesses of the garage. I left the cockroach culling to Steve, but one day I happened to go into the garage just after he had sprayed repellent around. It had the desired effect: there, at about 100 miles an hour, emerged a cockroach. It headed straight for me and I froze in absolute horror, while marvelling at its speed.

"Kill it!" yelled a frenzied Steve. "Stamp on it!"

Having already established that I only kill wasps, I must take a second to review that and extend my murderous intentions to include cockroaches. However, there was no power on this earth that could induce me to stand on one intentionally. *Oh, God!* It would crack and squish, and there would be all that yucky, giant, beastly mess. Besides, I had my sparkly, blue, peep toe shoes on. Why would anyone wish to get squashed cockroach on any shoe, let alone a sparkly, sequinned one? So with that in mind, I let out a loud squeal and beat a hasty retreat out of the garage. Behind me, I could hear Steve raging.

"Oh, great!" he declared. "Now it's gone under the unit. Thanks a lot!"

Steve waged a constant battle with leaky windows, draughty doors and multi-various other niggling problems in the different places we lived. Although many apartments in Malta and Gozo are beautifully finished, an equal or greater number of them are badly finished. They have wobbly sinks, toilets that do not flush properly and wonky handles on all kitchen units. That drove Steve mad.

Two days after we had moved into our third home, we told our landlord about the toilet that did not flush. He came around, lifted the lid off the cistern, stuck his hand into the water and pulled the lever.

"See?" he said as if addressing a small child. "That's all that's required."

Words absolutely failed me, but only for a few seconds as I explained the glaringly obvious in that neither Steve nor I wished to stick our hands into the cistern each time we had to flush it. That explanation did not seem to have occurred to the landlord. He looked puzzled and advised us that we could buy the necessary parts from the shop in town, to alleviate the problem.

"But it's your responsibility," I argued. "We've only just moved in and it's never worked."

The landlord then drew my attention to the clause in the contract we had signed upon moving in, which stated that the first 100 euros of any repairs or breakdown were the responsibility of the tenant. *Now*, words failed us! *What a great way to get your repairs done! Pass them on to unsuspecting tenants.* You have all been forewarned: always read the small print.

One unfortunate day, Steve's frustrations with the poor workmanship in the house in which we lived came to a head. The rain had poured in, in torrents, under the door and soaked all the rugs and furnishings. Steve was attempting to seal the cracks, but it was going all wrong. After seven years together, I had become pretty good at reading the signs and knew that a blow-up of volcanic proportions was imminent. I tried making myself scarce and got busy in the kitchen, but could hear the rumblings and mutterings increasing as everything went wrong. As I suspected, Steve erupted within 10 minutes, hurled the offending sealant down and yelled:

"Just bring me 40 euros and a box of matches, will you?"

Even though I knew how eccentric Steve could be, that seemed like an unusual request, so I went over.

"40 euros and a box of matches?" I repeated. "Whatever for?" I continued, fascinated.

"Because it's cheaper than me having to keep buying stuff and trying to sort this mess out," Steve fumed. "I may as well just burn the money and get it over with."

I had to admit it: he had a point.

Living in Żebbuġ, which is one of the highest villages, if not *the* highest village, in the small island of Gozo, we soon discovered that in addition to the stunning, 360-degree views and breath-taking scenery, we had to content with almost constant high winds. We only discovered after we moved there that Żebbuġ is known locally at the 'windy city' – for good reason. Not that it mattered in summer, because the wind kept us cool, but in winter, it got really cold. The wind also caused untold problems in blowing things around – things that usually ended up in the pool.

One day, I was chatting to my friend on the phone and looking out of the window at the same time. I had pegged my washing out on the line and was keeping an eye on it, because it was in real danger of taking off to Sicily on such a windy day. I had pegged the washing with every peg that I possessed, but it was still touch and go. As I talked on the phone, I peered out of the window. No, I could not see the washing. Not good; not good at all.

"Hang on, Pat," I said. "I'll have to go, I think my washing's blown away."

I shot outside and sure enough, the washing line had been overwhelmed, given way in the high winds and dumped all my almost dry washing into the deep end of the pool.

"Steve," I called, knowing that I would never be permitted to tackle such a task. "My washing's in the pool."

Steve emerged from the garage like a character from *The Hobbit*.

"Why is your washing in the pool?" he asked, quizzically, blinking in the light.

"The line broke," I explained.

Steve stood there, silently weighing in the situation. I tried to look helpful and stepped forward, grabbing the corner of my sinking duvet cover. It could not be socks and pants, could it?

"No, no," he shouted. "Leave it, I'll sort it out."

Clearly, it was not a job for a woman. It obviously required a man to fish washing out of a pool. Steve got his pool scoopy thing and began to fish around, hauling all the soaking sheets and duvet cover out as I stood by, admiring his skills and murmuring encouragement. Naturally, the washing all had to be cleaned up again and Steve had to put up another washing line, but he was not going to be caught out again. After some musing, wandering around and several long intakes of breath, Steve identified a proposed site, thought about it for a few hours, then happy with his decision, he relocated the line closer to the house where the winds were not quite as ferocious.

"There," he said in satisfaction. "That should do it."

Sure enough, the newly secured line never failed, but lasted for the duration of our stay. Steve's DIY skills had saved the day once again. A few months later, we endured seemingly endless days of gale force winds. For the first time in the four years we had been on the island, the Gozo ferry had to turn back to Malta as it could not dock due to the heavy seas. Even with the newly relocated washing line, I dared not peg anything out.

One night, we went to bed listening to the winds batter the tiny island and snuggled down gratefully under the covers. I must digress here to say that due to the damp, rain, leaks and so on, we had moved the bed downstairs. I had been upstairs in bed one morning when I felt a splash of water on my face. *What the ****?* I sat up and discovered that the heavy rain had found a way in through the ceiling. It was the last straw.

"It's raining on my face," I complained in a loud voice to a sleeping Steve. "I'm not happy about this," I continued as he opened one eye to see what was going on. "I mean, I shouldn't be in bed getting rained on," I said, finally. "It's not right."

Steve sleepily agreed and suggested that, while unconventional, he could move the bed downstairs as there was so much rain at the time.

"I love that idea," I enthused. "I mean, what's not to like?"

Thus it was that we moved the bed downstairs. We felt like Grandpa Jo and Grandma Josephine out of *Charlie and the Chocolate Factory*. On one level, it was ridiculous, but on another level it was highly convenient for watching the telly in bed – oh, and if you wanted a drink in the night: boom; already there! We secretly liked it, but got some funny looks from friends who called around, when they saw the bed in the living room. Mind you, I do not think they were *that* surprised – after all, it was us.

Anyway, there we were one night, sound asleep, when we heard *Bang, Bang, Bang* coming from the roof. Steve awoke instantly in combat mode.

"What? What?" he said as he became fully awake. "What is it?"

I half expected him to duck and roll at the tone of his voice. Now, whenever Steve got into a deep sleep, it was never a great idea to wake him up suddenly, especially without a lot of warning. So I would usually go for some gently whispered, "Steve, Steve," or a small, pointed prod to his shoulder. He was extremely cross, therefore, at having been so rudely awakened and even more cross when he realised that the noise was coming from the roof. What was happening meant that he would have to get dressed, arm himself with manly tools, climb onto the roof and survey the situation. It was a great shame that he did not have night vision goggles as I felt they would have added greatly to the situation.

No matter. Off Steve went, armed with tools and muttering bad temperedly to himself. I was still snug in bed, but felt that I could, at least, show some willingness and offer my assistance.

"Do you need me at all?" I asked, hoping the answer would be 'no.'

"You'd better come and make sure I'm OKAY!" came back the reply. "Make sure I don't fall."

Hmm, that sounded like a great responsibility. I reluctantly left the warmth of the bed and duly followed Steve up. I was immediately struck by the ferocity of the wind, which was indeed at gale force. Steve deduced that the problem was the lid of the water tank, which had come loose. He startled me by springing up onto a high wall. If he fell, he would land about 20 feet down on the terrace. I was terrified and grabbed Steve's belt, shouting out obvious warnings.

"For God's sake, be careful!" I shouted, repeatedly.

I was not as well prepared as Steve and had gone up onto the roof in my pink, fluffy dressing gown. Bad idea. My gown flapped around in the wind and I was grateful that it was highly unlikely anyone was watching. However, it placed Steve in even more danger. As he balanced himself precariously on the wall, banging around as cross as ever, I was hanging on for grim death, while being distracted by my dressing gown and spending almost as much time holding onto it.

"I'll have to drill it," said Steve, eventually.

I detected a quiet note of satisfaction in that further action was required. Of course, Steve had gone onto the roof fully equipped for such an eventuality. It was even more nail biting as he leaned back to get some purchase on the drill, so I abandoned all plans for retaining my dignity. I closed my eyes and hung fast to Steve's leather belt, wondering all the time what I would do if he actually fell. I knew that, in reality, I was nowhere near strong enough to prevent my husband from falling, but repeatedly tried to put the thought out of my mind. Finally, after a bit of high altitude drilling, the job was done and Steve could get down. I could regain my dignity. Subsequently, there was the mandatory muttering and cursing about stupid, badly made, badly designed water tanks, plus questions regarding their location and so on. But overall, Steve was satisfied with his handiwork.

We sank gratefully back into bed and I listened patiently for another few minutes to Steve's ideas for more efficient water tank designs, before falling asleep. Half an hour later, I was rudely awakened again as *Clunk!* – the humane mousetrap went off. I groaned. One of the problems in sleeping cosily downstairs was that even though we no longer got rained on in bed – a real plus – I could hear the result immediately if we snagged a mouse. That meant I then had to get up and liberate it, otherwise we could hear it gnawing and scratching as it tried to escape. Oddly, it always seemed to me that Steve tended to remain in a particularly deep sleep at such times as he never heard the mice. *Hmm, funny.* His hearing was usually razor sharp. Many's the time he heard a comment made at a gig from a whole room away over a background of music and talking, yet a mouse trap going off in the dead of the night eluded him. *Go figure!*

I gingerly picked up the trap with the mouse and made for the door, making many more loud noises as I opened it. I lived in constant fear of any trapped mice escaping, before I actually got to the end of the terrace where I let them go, so there I was in the high winds, poised with trap in hand. It was a bit tricky opening it, but eventually I managed it. Unfortunately, at precisely that moment in time, a particularly strong gust of wind arose that blew the mouse back in my direction. Happy to be free, the rodent ran up my arm and away over my shoulder!

You know that saying from the movie *Alien* whereby *In space, no one can hear you scream?* Well, I bet they heard me all the way up to the space station. *NOW* Steve was awake.

CHAPTER 32

Despite its unrivalled position overlooking the sea and despite all its charms, we knew that we could not stay in our current home at the time. With a disinterested landlord who did not care that it rained in and who told us that 80% dry was acceptable in a house, startlingly high utility bills and the almost non-stop barking of neighbourhood dogs, we knew that we would not be able to tolerate another summer. There was also the added problem of next door – a holiday let. We had been untruthfully told that it was only rented out in July and August, when we had first viewed the house. The rest of the time, we had been assured, we would not have any neighbours, so we would (presumably) enjoy peace and quiet most of the year. But we soon realised that the house next door was let out almost constantly.

Gozo has many festivals and many Maltese cross over to enjoy them, so while many Maltese have their own property, many others rent out farmhouses for the long weekends of celebrations. The house next door was no exception and unfortunately for us, it could sleep up to 20 people and seemed to be let out most weekends. We were initially awakened to the shape of things to come when we were about to go to bed one night. We heard the sound of cars pulling up, then a lot of scraping and banging next door.

"Looks like we've got company," said Steve, eyeing the walls from whence the noise came, grimacing.

The following morning we realised just how much company we had when a gang of about 12 young lads piled out onto the pool terrace, turned their music up to 'deafen and stun,' and began to party. I stared at Steve in horror.

"It's nine o'clock in the morning," I said in disbelief. "I'm not putting up with a racket like this at nine o'clock in the morning!"

I got dressed and went downstairs to investigate further. I looked over the boundary wall and sure enough, there was a group of lads all in their 20's. The music was absolutely ear splitting, but one of the words I had usefully learned in Maltese was the word for "turn it down."

"Hey, you lot. *Baxxilu!*" I yelled over the wall.

They did not hear me above the din. I repeated myself, louder. One of the lads heard me and nudged his friends. They all turned to stare at the wild-eyed Englishwoman who was clearly upset and yelling at them to turn their music down. With a shrug, they complied for all of 10 minutes, before the volume crept back up. I tolerated it for about half an hour before marching around to their door and hammering on it for at least five more minutes, until they finally heard it above the noise. A disinterested youth stood in front of me and raised an insolent eyebrow. I got straight to the point.

"I live here," I said flatly, "and I am not putting up with this noise all weekend, so turn it down or I will call the police."

He said nothing, but shut the door ignorantly in my face. Steve had a better idea.

"I'll connect my speakers and put them outside," he said, angrily. "Let's see how they like 1000 watts of *Whitesnake* in their ears."

But we knew it was not to way to go and would only start trouble, so instead we retreated inside and fumed in silence.

That situation was pretty much the pattern for the whole summer. We would dread hearing the crunch of car tyres as they pulled up and we had given up on asking people to keep the noise down as they took no notice whatsoever. The police told us that they had been in touch with the owner of the house and warned him, to no avail. He lived in Malta, so he was unaffected by the inconvenience and the noise, and was undoubtedly making a huge amount of money out of it all. After one particularly horrendous weekend where the noise had continued unabated until

4.00am, Steve commented that, in his opinion, the place was being used for drug taking and partying, and no one gave a damn. He declared that as soon as our rental agreement came to an end, we were moving. I felt saddened. We had not expected that in sleepy, little Gozo. It felt more like a busy city centre, with drunken revellers and ignorant people, but I knew that Steve was right. We could not put up with another year like that.

Things came to a head one day in February. It was the festival in Nadur – one of the main feasts on the island. We knew that people would cross over in their thousands and braced ourselves for a noisy weekend. On the day in question, we had intentionally gone out to the shops at around 8.00am. When we returned, we were annoyed to find six cars parked in the full length of our driveway, blocking our way and preventing us from parking. I got out of the car and collared a young man who was wandering around.

"You can't park here," I explained. "We have to be able to park and our neighbours need to be able to get their vehicle out and you're blocking them in," I said, pointing to our next door-but-one neighbour's truck, which was effectively imprisoned at the end of the line of trespassing cars.

The young man agreed to move his car and we went inside, muttering about the onslaught of partygoers who would, no doubt, keep us awake into the small hours of the morning. It was at that point that our neighbours came around. They too were horrified at the influx of the latest gang of young people who, by their reckoning, were 20-strong and had piled into the house laden with beer and spirits. We were definitely in for a noisy one. Our neighbour told us that he was about to go around and ask them to move all the cars, so that he could get his truck out. Less than five minutes later, he was back, his eyes wide open.

"Listen," he said in an urgent whisper. "The guy who came to the door said he was a police officer. He told me I'd have to wait. What do you think's going on?" he asked us.

Steve looked at me, knowingly.

"It's drugs," he said bluntly. "I've said it all along, it's a drug house."

The drama continued when a few minutes later the police officer came to our door to explain what was going on. It was exactly as Steve had said. Apparently, the group of young people had been followed from Malta to Gozo, after a tip-off regarding them carrying drugs. The police had followed them to this particular house and conducted a raid. There was a thorough search, resulting in half the young people being arrested and charged with drug offences. It made the local headlines and succeeded in bringing over the owner from Malta.

Upon entering the house after the weekend, the owner discovered that it had been well and truly trashed. His plasma TV had been ripped off the wall, beds were broken, the telephone had been pulled out and there was, apparently, wall-to-wall rubbish that required a truck to remove it all. All that from one group of kids. The young people were released on bail and returned to the house, unrepentant. At midnight, we had to call the police out to stop the noise, which they did temporarily, but they soon started again. By 6.00am, after hours of listening to non-stop *Boom, Boom, Boom,* we decided it was the last straw. We rang up our landlord and told him that we would not be renewing our contract. We were on the move yet again and for a short time, the grass seemed sadly the same shade as it had done in England.

After the weekend of the drug bust, we began looking for a suitable property in which to live. We mentioned it to a friend who, by chance, happened to know someone who was looking for tenants, for his four bedroom farmhouse in the village of Xagħra. We arranged a viewing and were immediately struck by the newness of the house, which was only two years old. The owners had taken great care in building it. It was clean, bright, modern and best of all, free from damp, mould and leaks. The place had three floors, amazing views of the island from the roof and sun terrace, lots of space, air conditioning, a garage and a swimming pool.

We laughed as we had said that we would never have another pool, but it was smaller and less high maintenance than the previous pool, and we agreed that it would certainly be nice in summer. A deal was struck and we agreed to move into the new house as soon as our old contract expired, which was in seven weeks. The time could not go by fast enough.

We instantly began the tedious task of packing up our belongings once again. This time, however, we did not have nearly as much stuff, thanks to our success in selling items on *Maltapark* and at the car boot sales. This time we would not need a removal firm, but could manage with the help of good friends and neighbours. Our new landlord generously agreed that we could start moving in our stuff in two weeks before our official move-in date, allowing us to move in an organised fashion. As we shifted more and more things to the new house, my little dream house, which had turned into an emptied nightmare, I could not help but feel sad. I had so wanted to stay in the beautifully appointed house by the sea, but it was not to be.

I thought I would pine for the views, the wildness of its high vantage point where I used to love standing and letting the wind whip up my hair, but I knew that the poor condition of the place, coupled with the noise and trouble next door far outweighed the benefits. So with more than a little regret, I said goodbye to the house that had appeared in my dreams so many years ago and realised that while dreams do sometimes come true, they are not necessarily good dreams. Our move to Xagħra went smoothly and the first night in our new home was spent marvelling at the silence. We awoke to bright sunshine streaming through the windows and knew, without a doubt, that we had made the right decision.

Another billboard

CHAPTER 33

June 2014

I t is now mid-June and I am walking up the hill from the seaside town of Marsalforn, to the hilltop village of Xagħra. Behind me, the sea is a stunning blanket of sparkling diamond chips, like shattered ice on glass. The temperature is hovering around the 29-degree mark and I am thankful for the fairly strong wind that is blowing from Africa to this little island of Gozo. It affords me some relief as I make my way up to the village in which we are now living, our fourth home on the island in as many years. The wind blows with some intent through the tall stems of sweet corn growing in many allotments along the way. The noise of the tall, woody stems rattling together is all I can hear; it is strangely comforting. The fronds of the wild fennel plants sway in the breeze, inviting me to inhale their scent. I stop briefly and crush a few leaves between my fingers, enjoying the fragrance of the offered aniseed.

Above me flies a lone buzzard making silent, lazy circles in the baby blue sky. I see it and urge it onwards, hoping that it will not fall foul of one of the many hunters who will shoot it pointlessly out of the sky in the name of sport. Geckos and lizards dart around my feet, disturbed as I make my way up the long hill, disappearing into cracks in the walls. A sudden flash of black alerts me to the presence of a whip snake in the hedge. In a fluid, beautiful movement, the snake moves unhurriedly out of my path, all four feet of its graceful, lithe body sliding out of sight in an instant. I am not alarmed; it offers no threat.

Occasionally, the peace of day is interrupted by a passing tractor carrying a farmer to his allotment or field. They nod and smile as they pass by on their ancient machines, which would not look out of place in post-war Britain. *Bonġu!* they call as they pass me by and I return the greeting and smile. The taste of the old tractor's diesel fumes stays with me momentarily after they pass.

I can hear my breathing getting slightly more laboured as I continue on my way back home. I question my decision to go walking at such a foolish hour, given the strength of the sun. I was tricked by the wind into thinking it would not be too hot. I was wrong. I make a mental note to take my daily walk much earlier in future, now that summer is finally here. Looking up the hill, I see the *Cornucopia Hotel* where Steve and I got married in 2011, and the memory of that day brings a smile to my face. I find that I have much to smile about, living on this magical island. It seemed a long time ago since that first holiday, which had been so fraught with stress and tension. *Was it only four years ago that we made our first visit here?*

Ten more minutes of concentrated effort gets me to the top of the hill where I rest for a while on one of the conveniently placed benches. From here, I have an unparalleled and glorious view of the sea, which acts as a reward for my efforts. I gaze at this splendid scene in awe and know that I will never grow bored of it. Rested, I make my way the 100 yards into the village shop, pushing through the plastic fronds that act as a barrier against the heat and mosquitos. Its small, unassuming frontage belies the surprisingly large, well-stocked, cool interior.

"Morning, Maria," I call out to the owner.

I am met with a welcoming smile of recognition and pleasure. I am immediately chastened by Maria who puts down her sweeping broom.

"You have been walking," she says in a reproving tone.

It is a statement, not a question.

"It's too hot to walk. You must wait until it's cooler," Maria scolds.

I immediately acknowledge her wisdom and agree that I will walk earlier in the morning, in future. We exchange pleasantries, discuss our husbands and their mutual love of sweet things, agree that they must be limited in that regard and laugh about it together. I buy my groceries and am treated with the utmost politeness and respect.

"Come again and have a good day," says Maria as I leave.

We both know that I will. It is but a tiny part of my day, but one that adds to the feeling of belonging I have, solidifying my affinity with this island and its people. I walk the scant half-mile home, past the house where the group of wild-eyed, feral cats are congregating to be fed by the elderly lady within. They regard me with stiff-legged suspicion and stalk away, waiting until I am safely out of their territory, before returning to await their only meal of the day. *What will they do when she's gone?* I wonder with a tinge of sadness.

I am home. I open the door and step into the cool interior of our latest home.

"I'm back," I call to Steve.

From somewhere up in the music room, his guitar playing is interrupted as Steve calls out his acknowledgement upon hearing this news.

"You okay?" he asks.

I think about this question. *Am I okay?* I was home. Home in Gozo where, despite the ups and downs we had experienced in our four years here, the grass was greener that I had ever imagined it could be. Home to the man who loved and cared for me in a way I had never imagined possible; who was, without a doubt, the love of my life and who had shown me just how green the grass could, indeed, be.

"Yes," I call back with a contented smile. "I'm okay."

And I truly was.

Freya, Steve and Ollie after the wedding

EPILOGUE

In 2015, Steve and I moved from Gozo to the south of France, so that I could write the sequel to my debut novel *Known to Social Services.* Within a few days after its release, *Known to Social Services* had become the #1 UK Bestseller in the Social Work category for books. We will, however, be returning to the beautiful and beloved island of Gozo on a regular basis.

First dance as husband and wife

ABOUT THE AUTHOR

Freya Barrington is the pen name of the author of *Known to Social Services*, the #1 UK Bestseller in the Social Work Category for early 2015. This book titled *Gozo: Is the Grass Greener?* is her second work. Freya grew up in Lancashire, England with an overriding passion for animals, specifically horses. After attending girls grammar school where English was her strongest subject, the only desire Freya held was to work with her beloved horses. To the dismay of her parents, she went to work in a racing yard.

Realising that it was not a passing phase, her parents eventually encouraged Freya in her chosen career and she went on to work with event horses, show jumpers and hunters, gaining several *British Horse Society* qualifications along the way – namely, the BHSAI, BHSII and BHSI (SM). All this enabled Freya to work as a riding instructor and trainer, which she did on a freelance basis. Freya continued working in the equestrian field for many years, eventually running her own yard.

A chance conversation with a friend brought about a change of career for Freya and she moved away from her life with horses, into the unknown world of residential childcare. To her surprise, Freya found that she enjoyed that line of work and progressed to being a full-time foster carer for the local authority. It was at that time Freya first put pen to paper in a creative way, writing poems about the children with whom she came into contact. A short book of poetry was soon published and the proceeds were used to raise money for a local youth group.

During her time as a foster carer, Freya came into contact with social workers. Their dedication and expertise inspired her to also train as a social worker, gaining the Diploma in Social Work in 2001 from the University of Derby, with an award for excellence in practice. Freya also gained the Post-Qualifying Award in 2007. She is a registered member in good standing with the Health and Care Professions Council (HCPC) of the United Kingdom.

The main area of expertise of Freya Barrington is as a senior child protection social worker. She has been the principal social worker and mentor on a number of teams. Freya has also worked as a foster carer's support social worker, as a court advisor and hospital social worker. Since 2006, Freya has worked exclusively as an agency social worker, with specific focus on working for local authorities that require experienced social workers to offer support in the face of staff shortages. Freya's assessments and reports are in high demand, with managers from several local authority areas making specific requests for her to join their teams.

In 2010, Freya moved with her husband, Steve, to the island of Gozo (Maltese Islands). Meanwhile, she continued working in England as an agency social worker, flying back and forth on a fortnightly basis. This attracted comments from colleagues who said that they would never again complain about their commute to work! It was at that time that the idea for writing her nonfiction books started taking shape, so with the full support of her husband, Freya took a year's sabbatical to write.

Freya lived in Gozo with her husband from 2010 to mid-2015. It is the experiences they went through in this small, beautiful island in the Mediterranean that are presented in her second book titled *Gozo: Is the*

Grass Greener? Freya is presently in the south of France, writing the sequel to *Known to Social Services*.

More about Freya Barrington and her work can be found at:
- *Amazon* http://www.amazon.co.uk/Freya-Barrington/e/B00U228K5I/ref=ntt_athr_dp_pel_1
- *Blog* freyabarrington.blogspot.com
- *Facebook Page* facebook.com/FreyaBarrington
- *Twitter* @freyabarrington
- *Google+* plus.google.com/107614255402573788705/posts

SELECTED FARAXA PUBLICATIONS

Written from life experience and ringing with authenticity, the **#1 UK Bestseller in the Social Work Category** for early 2015, *Known to Social Services* by Freya Barrington follows Diane Foster, a dedicated social worker, into the grim, grey world of the Deacon Hill estate in Millbrook and the tormented lives of its inhabitants. Domestic violence, child abuse, serial paedophiles and ex-convicts proliferate in the daily lives of most of the children, but Diane enters deeply into this world of misery to help the victims and keep together the fragile structure of society. Hampered by an administration inhabited by paper-shuffling and uninvolved, uncaring bureaucrats, Diane fights unremittingly to protect the children of Deacon Hill from rape, horror, random violence, female genital mutilation and murder, within the context of a horrifying barrenness and desolate existential reality.

Bonds in the Mirror of Time is a psychological novel by Rena Balzan, Ph.D., translated from the original Maltese by Antoinette Pace. Love and selfishness continually compete with each other, dominating the lives of the protagonists. Why was Nada abandoned by Erica when both needed each other? Who was Maris? Why was Claud dating her when he loved Nada? The painter was afraid to fulfil himself as an artist. Why did he end his relationship with Erica, the woman who desired to help him succeed at all cost? In this novel, the human bonding that exists

between the protagonists is not necessarily annihilated by death. On the contrary, the psychological barriers death portrays present a challenge for overcoming them.

The Legend of Amanda Robins for young adults by 14-year-old Corrine Annette Zahra. A fast-moving, gripping account of the turmoil due to the destruction of Magic State, an invisible island north of Australia. Queen Amanda is forced to evacuate her land and send the inhabitants to live with humankind. Her ex-husband, Dylan, has escaped from prison with hordes of werewolves and launched a vicious attack. From the streets of New York where new Twin Towers are born, to the White House, Queen Amanda puts all her powers on display. War and intrigue permeate the pages of Zahra's book which should prove un-put-downable for lovers of magical creatures.

A Land in the Storytelling Sea – A North American in Malta by Sheryl Loeffler presents 50 poems and 50 full-colour, original photographs of the Maltese Islands. Sensual, painterly, even prayerful, these poems and pictures deepen into a land of legend and myth; an island populated, past and present, by saints, beggars and pirates, all of whom are blessed by vivid geometries of light. Loeffler portrays Malta as a country awash in splendour and contradiction, a "land where Christians call God *Alla.*" Quietly pleasurable in narrative journey and in its subtle, seductive craft.

The Battle Roar of Silence – Foucault and the Carceral System by Meinrad Calleja explores the philosophical rationales sustaining morality, law, punishment and the carceral system as part of the discourse of globalization. Calleja attempts to desacralize the foundations of this discourse using Foucault's archaeological and genealogical study of institutions, knowledge, discourse and power. This is an interdisciplinary study fusing aspects of sociology and psychoanalysis within a philosophical framework, to tender a politically-charged critique of the contemporary modes of domination and power. Calleja correlates the carceral system discourse to political, social and economic antagonisms that have eroded human rights,  democracy and freedom. Consumers of this discourse repress the negative features of such a despotic order and suffer in silence. Articulated is the battle roar of silence.

Popular Operas in the Maltese Islands by Maltese, award-winning author Tony C. Cutajar presents the 20 most favourite operas from the time they started being produced in Malta and Gozo up to 2012. Almost all operas were sentimental or tragic, lyric operas. Interesting details about each opera and its composer are given, together with plot summaries. Interactive links to audio/video selections of the best arias are also provided in the ebook edition of this book.

Bormla – A Struggling Community is a landmark study in which JosAnn Cutajar, Ph.D., presents the people's situation in this impoverished, historical city in Malta. Communities living in places stigmatized by policy makers, the media and the general population, develop coping skills to acquire alternative resources for their social well-being. In Maltese society, resources are often deployed by policy and decision makers not cognizant of the differential needs of communities living in different places. Cutajar gives voice to the people of Bormla, brings their needs to the forefront and gives effective recommendations for change.

Ricasoli Soldier – A Novel Inspired by True Events by Maltese-French author Joe Scicluna presents the historical story of Leo Bonanno, a young man who left Sicily in 1806 to enlist as a soldier with the British Army in Malta. The British had just formed the new regiment and recruited many from Albania, Greece, Italy, Russia and Turkey. But the recruitment process was fraudulent, with many becoming enlisted without informed consent. Leo held many hopes, dreams and ambitions of youth, including the desire to become a soldier to better serve his country. Stationed at Fort Ricasoli in Malta, Leo made new friends and fell madly in love with Lisa, a beautiful village girl from Kalkara. But all Leo's hopes, dreams and ambitions rapidly

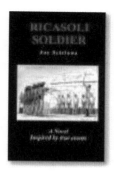

turned into a terrifying nightmare and incomparable battle for survival, due to a system of iniquity imposed by a major who was a heartless tyrant.

The Adventures of Joe Fenek by Graham Bayes is the winner of an honorable mention at the 2013 London Book Festival. This book for children presents six stories about Joe Fenek – Joe the Rabbit. Meet Joe and his animal friends Jimmy the rat, Digger the shrew, Tony the rat, Horace the horse, Mario the mouse and Spikey the hedgehog,, all of which share in Joe's adventures around Malta and Gozo.

Strange Tales (Combined Illustrated Ed.) by Charles Coyne is a collection of 29 short horror stories, many of which are set in the Maltese Islands. Ranging from Max the doll who ends up being a preternatural killer, through Meinertzhagen the man who turns into a boy after death who tries to entrap his best friend, to Loki the shaman who visits with the dead, Coyne keeps his readers on edge, gripping the seat of their chairs, both during the telling of the tales and in their surprise endings.

Escape: A Supernatural Serial for young adults by Corrine Annette Zahra. I am Tiffany Crooks and live with my little sister, Minnie, at *The Turville's* with Grandma Crooks. But who are the Crooks and the Turvilles? Why does Grandma Crooks want to consecrate my sister with blood to the dark sacred, even though we are Christian? Who is the flame-flickered hound? Why did our parents disappear after they had dropped us off with Grandma Crooks? Where are they now? What is going to happen to us?

The Philosophy of Desert Metaphors in Ibrahim al-Koni – The Bleeding of the Stone by Meinrad Calleja takes a close look at one of al-Koni's works, prising out philosophical reflections in the text. A Tuareg by birth, al-Koni is no longer an emerging author. His works have earned him international repute and academic recognition. Themed around a desert context, his novels are post-modern, polyphonic, magical or socialist realism and Sufi fabula. In this book, Calleja shows how the desert provides a landscape rich in allusions, while metaphors allow readers to engage in creative interpretation.

Stories My Parents Told Me – Tales of Growing Up in Wartime Malta are seven stories by Rupert C. Grech, based on actual events during WWII in Malta. Grech skillfully shows the difficult time it was for children and families, where survival was paramount and family ties were what sustained them. The stories are interspersed with snippets of history, factual details and settings for tales emotionally moving, some of which bring a smile to your face. Grech also describes a culture of a time past for a deeply religious, frugal people.

Made in the USA
Charleston, SC
20 July 2015